MEMORIES AND STUDIES

MEMORIES AND STUDIES

BY

WILLIAM JAMES

GREENWOOD PRESS, PUBLISHERS
NEW YORK   1968

Reprinted with the permission of
David McKay Company, Inc.

LIBRARY OF CONGRESS catalogue card number: 68-19276

Printed in the United States of America

PREFATORY NOTE

Professor William James formed the intention shortly before his death of republishing a number of popular addresses and essays under the title which this book now bears; but unfortunately he found no opportunity to attend to any detail of the book himself, or to leave definite instructions for others. I believe, however, that I have departed in no substantial degree from my father's idea, except perhaps by including two or three short pieces which were first addressed to special occasions or audiences and which now seem clearly worthy of republication in their original form, although he might not have been willing to reprint them himself without the recastings to which he was ever most attentive when preparing for new readers. Everything in this volume has already appeared in print in magazines or otherwise, and definite acknowledgements are hereinafter made in the appropriate places. Comparison with the original texts will disclose slight variations in a few passages, and it is therefore proper to explain that in these passages the present text follows emendations of the original which have survived in the author's own handwriting.

Henry James, Jr.

CONTENTS

I
LOUIS AGASSIZ

I

LOUIS AGASSIZ[1]

It would be unnatural to have such an assemblage as this meet in the Museum and Faculty Room of this University and yet have no public word spoken in honor of a name which must be silently present to the minds of all our visitors.

At some near future day, it is to be hoped some one of you who is well acquainted with Agassiz's scientific career will discourse here concerning it, — I could not now, even if I would, speak to you of that of which you have far more intimate knowledge than I. On this social occasion it has seemed that what Agassiz stood for in the way of character and influence is the more fitting thing to commemorate, and to that agreeable task I have been called. He made an impression that was

[1] Words spoken at the reception of the American Society of Naturalists by the President and Fellows of Harvard College at Cambridge, December 30, 1896. Printed in *Science*, N. S. V. 285.

unrivalled. He left a sort of popular myth — the Agassiz legend, as one might say — behind him in the air about us; and life comes kindlier to all of us, we get more recognition from the world, because we call ourselves naturalists, — and that was the class to which he also belonged.

The secret of such an extraordinarily effective influence lay in the equally extraordinary mixture of the animal and social gifts, the intellectual powers, and the desires and passions of the man. From his boyhood, he looked on the world as if it and he were made for each other, and on the vast diversity of living things as if he were there with authority to take mental possession of them all. His habit of collecting began in childhood, and during his long life knew no bounds save those that separate the things of Nature from those of human art. Already in his student years, in spite of the most stringent poverty, his whole scheme of existence was that of one predestined to greatness, who takes that fact for granted, and stands

4

forth immediately as a scientific leader of men.

His passion for knowing living things was combined with a rapidity of observation, and a capacity to recognize them again and remember everything about them, which all his life it seemed an easy triumph and delight for him to exercise, and which never allowed him to waste a moment in doubts about the commensurability of his powers with his tasks. If ever a person lived by faith, he did. When a boy of twenty, with an allowance of two hundred and fifty dollars a year, he maintained an artist attached to his employ, a custom which never afterwards was departed from, — except when he maintained two or three. He lectured from the very outset to all those who would hear him. "I feel within myself the strength of a whole generation," he wrote to his father at that time, and launched himself upon the publication of his costly "Poissons Fossiles" with no clear vision of the quarter from whence the payment might be expected to come.

At Neuchâtel (where between the ages of twenty-five and thirty he enjoyed a stipend that varied from four hundred to six hundred dollars) he organized a regular academy of natural history, with its museum, managing by one expedient or another to employ artists, secretaries, and assistants, and to keep a lithographic and printing establishment of his own employed with the work that he put forth. Fishes, fossil and living, echinoderms and glaciers, transfigured themselves under his hand, and at thirty he was already at the zenith of his reputation, recognized by all as one of those naturalists in the unlimited sense, one of those folio copies of mankind, like Linnæus and Cuvier, who aim at nothing less than an acquaintance with the whole of animated Nature. His genius for classifying was simply marvellous; and, as his latest biographer says, nowhere had a single person ever given so decisive an impulse to natural history.

Such was the human being who on an October morning fifty years ago disembarked

at our port, bringing his hungry heart along
with him, his confidence in his destiny, and
his imagination full of plans. The only particular resource he was assured of was one
course of Lowell Lectures. But of one general resource he always was assured, having
always counted on it and never found it to
fail, — and that was the good will of every
fellow-creature in whose presence he could
find an opportunity to describe his aims. His
belief in these was so intense and unqualified
that he could not conceive of others not feeling the furtherance of them to be a duty
binding also upon them. *Velle non discitur*,
as Seneca says: — Strength of desire must be
born with a man, it can't be taught. And
Agassiz came before one with such enthusiasm
glowing in his countenance, — such a persuasion radiating from his person that his
projects were the sole things really fit to interest man as man, — that he was absolutely
irresistible. He came, in Byron's words, with
victory beaming from his breast, and every
one went down before him, some yielding him

7

money, some time, some specimens, and some labor, but all contributing their applause and their godspeed. And so, living among us from month to month and from year to year, with no relation to prudence except his pertinacious violation of all her usual laws, he on the whole achieved the compass of his desires, studied the geology and fauna of a continent, trained a generation of zoölogists, founded one of the chief museums of the world, gave a new impulse to scientific education in America, and died the idol of the public, as well as of his circle of immediate pupils and friends.

The secret of it all was, that while his scientific ideals were an integral part of his being, something that he never forgot or laid aside, so that wherever he went he came forward as "the Professor," and talked "shop" to every person, young or old, great or little, learned or unlearned, with whom he was thrown, he was at the same time so commanding a presence, so curious and inquiring, so responsive and expansive, and so generous

8

and reckless of himself and of his own, that every one said immediately, "Here is no musty *savant*, but a man, a great man, a man on the heroic scale, not to serve whom is avarice and sin." He elevated the popular notion of what a student of Nature could be. Since Benjamin Franklin, we had never had among us a person of more popularly impressive type. He did not wait for students to come to him; he made inquiry for promising youthful collectors, and when he heard of one, he wrote, inviting and urging him to come. Thus there is hardly one now of the American naturalists of my generation whom Agassiz did not train. Nay, more; he said to every one that a year or two of natural history, studied as he understood it, would give the best training for any kind of mental work. Sometimes he was amusingly *naïf* in this regard, as when he offered to put his whole Museum at the disposition of the Emperor of Brazil if he would but come and labor there. And I well remember how certain officials of the Brazilian empire smiled

9

at the cordiality with which he pressed upon them a similar invitation. But it had a great effect. Natural history must indeed be a godlike pursuit, if such a man as this can so adore it, people said; and the very definition and meaning of the word naturalist underwent a favorable alteration in the common mind.

Certain sayings of Agassiz's, as the famous one that he "had no time for making money," and his habit of naming his occupation simply as that of "teacher," have caught the public fancy, and are permanent benefactions. We all enjoy more consideration for the fact that he manifested himself here thus before us in his day.

He was a splendid example of the temperament that looks forward and not backward, and never wastes a moment in regrets for the irrevocable. I had the privilege of admission to his society during the Thayer expedition to Brazil. I well remember at night, as we all swung in our hammocks in the fairy-like moonlight, on the deck of the steamer that

10

throbbed its way up the Amazon between the forests guarding the stream on either side, how he turned and whispered, "James, are you awake?" and continued, "*I* cannot sleep; I am too happy; I keep thinking of these glorious plans." The plans contemplated following the Amazon to its headwaters, and penetrating the Andes in Peru. And yet, when he arrived at the Peruvian frontier and learned that that country had broken into revolution, that his letters to officials would be useless, and that that part of the project must be given up, although he was indeed bitterly chagrined and excited for part of an hour, when the hour had passed over it seemed as if he had quite forgotten the disappointment, so enthusiastically was he occupied already with the new scheme substituted by his active mind.

Agassiz's influence on methods of teaching in our community was prompt and decisive, — all the more so that it struck people's imagination by its very excess. The good old way of committing printed abstractions to memory seems never to have received such a shock as it encountered at his hands. There is probably no public school teacher now in New England who will not tell you how Agassiz used to lock a student up in a room full of turtle shells, or lobster shells, or oyster shells, without a book or word to help him, and not let him out till he had discovered all the truths which the objects contained. Some found the truths after weeks and months of lonely sorrow; others never found them. Those who found them were already made into naturalists thereby — the failures were blotted from the book of honor and of life. "Go to Nature; take the facts into your own hands; look, and see for yourself!"— these were the maxims which Agassiz preached wherever he went, and their effect on pedagogy was electric. The extreme rigor of his devotion to this concrete method of learning was the natural consequence of his own peculiar type of intellect, in which the capacity for abstraction and causal reasoning and tracing chains of consequences from hypoth-

eses was so much less developed than the
genius for acquaintance with vast volumes of
detail, and for seizing upon analogies and relations of the more proximate and concrete
kind. While on the Thayer expedition, I
remember that I often put questions to him
about the facts of our new tropical habitat,
but I doubt if he ever answered one of these
questions of mine outright. He always said:
"There, you see you have a definite problem;
go and look and find the answer for yourself."
His severity in this line was a living rebuke
to all abstractionists and would-be biological
philosophers. More than once have I heard
him quote with deep feeling the lines from
Faust:

" Grau, theurer Freund, ist alle Theorie.
   Und grun des Lebens goldner Baum."

The only man he really loved and had use
for was the man who could bring him facts.
To see facts, not to argue or *raisonniren*, was
what life meant for him; and I think he often
positively loathed the ratiocinating type of

mind. "Mr. Blank, you are *totally* uneducated!" I heard him once say to a student who propounded to him some glittering theoretic generality. And on a similar occasion he gave an admonition that must have sunk deep into the heart of him to whom it was addressed. "Mr. X, some people perhaps now consider you a bright young man; but when you are fifty years old, if they ever speak of you then, what they will say will be this: 'That X, — oh, yes, I know him; he used to be a very bright young man!'" Happy is the conceited youth who at the proper moment receives such salutary cold water therapeutics as this from one who, in other respects, is a kind friend. We cannot all escape from being abstractionists. I myself, for instance, have never been able to escape; but the hours I spent with Agassiz so taught me the difference between all possible abstractionists and all livers in the light of the world's concrete fulness, that I have never been able to forget it. Both kinds of mind have their place in the infinite

14

design, but there can be no question as to which kind lies the nearer to the divine type of thinking.

Agassiz's view of Nature was saturated with simple religious feeling, and for this deep but unconventional religiosity he found at Harvard the most sympathetic possible environment. In the fifty years that have sped since he arrived here our knowledge of Nature has penetrated into joints and recesses which his vision never pierced. The causal elements and not the totals are what we are now most passionately concerned to understand; and naked `and poverty-stricken enough do the stripped-out elements and forces occasionally appear to us to be. But the truth of things is after all their living fulness, and some day, from a more commanding point of view than was possible to any one in Agassiz's generation, our descendants, enriched with the spoils of all our analytic investigations, will get round again to that higher and simpler way of looking at Nature. Meanwhile as we look back upon Agassiz, there floats up a breath as of life's morning, that makes the world seem young and fresh once more. May we all, and especially may those younger members of our association who never knew him, give a grateful thought to his memory as we wander through that Museum which he founded, and through this University whose ideals he did so much to elevate and define.

II

ADDRESS AT THE EMERSON CENTENARY IN CONCORD

II

ADDRESS AT THE EMERSON CENTENARY IN CONCORD[1]

THE pathos of death is this, that when the days of one's life are ended, those days that were so crowded with business and felt so heavy in their passing, what remains of one in memory should usually be so slight a thing. The phantom of an attitude, the echo of a certain mode of thought, a few pages of print, some invention, or some victory we gained in a brief critical hour, are all that can survive the best of us. It is as if the whole of a man's significance had now shrunk into the phantom of an attitude, into a mere musical note or phrase suggestive of his singularity — happy are those whose singularity gives a note so clear as to be victorious over the inevitable pity of such a diminution and abridgment.

[1] An Address delivered at the Centenary of the Birth of Ralph Waldo Emerson in Concord, May 25, 1903, and printed in the published proceedings of that meeting.

An ideal wraith like this, of Emerson's personality, hovers over all Concord to-day, taking, in the minds of those of you who were his neighbors and intimates a somewhat fuller shape, remaining more abstract in the younger generation, but bringing home to all of us the notion of a spirit indescribably precious. The form that so lately moved upon these streets and country roads, or awaited in these fields and woods the beloved Muse's visits, is now dust; but the soul's note, the spiritual voice, rises strong and clear above the uproar of the times, and seems securely destined to exert an ennobling influence over future generations.

What gave a flavor so matchless to Emerson's individuality was, even more than his rich mental gifts, their singularly harmonious combination. Rarely has a man so accurately known the limits of his genius or so unfailingly kept within them. "Stand by your order," he used to say to youthful students; and perhaps the paramount impression one gets of his life is of his loyalty to his own personal type and mission. The type was that of what he liked to call the scholar, the perceiver of pure truth; and the mission was that of the reporter in worthy form of each perception. The day is good, he said, in which we have the most perceptions. There are times when the cawing of a crow, a weed, a snowflake, or a farmer planting in his field become symbols to the intellect of truths equal to those which the most majestic phenomena can open. Let me mind my own charge, then, walk alone, consult the sky, the field and forest, sedulously waiting every morning for the news concerning the structure of the universe which the good Spirit will give me.

This was the first half of Emerson, but only half; for genius, as he said, is insatiate for expression, and truth has to be clad in the right verbal garment. The form of the garment was so vital with Emerson that it is impossible to separate it from the matter. They form a chemical combination — thoughts which would be trivial expressed otherwise,

are important through the nouns and verbs
to which he married them. The style is the
man, it has been said; the man Emerson's
mission culminated in his style, and if we
must define him in one word, we have to call
him Artist. He was an artist whose medium
was verbal and who wrought in spiritual
material.

This duty of spiritual seeing and reporting
determined the whole tenor of his life. It
was to shield this duty from invasion and
distraction that he dwelt in the country, that
he consistently declined to entangle himself
with associations or to encumber himself with
functions which, however he might believe in
them, he felt were duties for other men and
not for him. Even the care of his garden,
"with its stoopings and fingerings in a few
yards of space," he found "narrowing and
poisoning," and took to long free walks
and saunterings instead, without apology.
"Causes" innumerable sought to enlist him as
their "worker" — all got his smile and word
of sympathy, but none entrapped him into

service. The struggle against slavery itself, deeply as it appealed to him, found him firm: "God must govern his own world, and knows his way out of this pit without my desertion of my post, which has none to guard it but me. I have quite other slaves to face than those Negroes, to wit, imprisoned thoughts far back in the brain of man, and which have no watchman or lover or defender but me." This in reply to the possible questions of his own conscience. To hot-blooded moralists with more objective ideas of duty, such a fidelity to the limits of his genius must often have made him seem provokingly remote and unavailable; but we, who can see things in more liberal perspective, must unqualifiably approve the results. The faultless tact with which he kept his safe limits while he so dauntlessly asserted himself within them, is an example fitted to give heart to other theorists and artists the world over.

The insight and creed from which Emerson's life followed can be best summed up in his own verses:

"So nigh is grandeur to our dust,
　So near is God to man!"

Through the individual fact there ever shone for him the effulgence of the Universal Reason. The great Cosmic Intellect terminates and houses itself in mortal men and passing hours. Each of us is an angle of its eternal vision, and the only way to be true to our Maker is to be loyal to ourselves. "O rich and various Man!" he cries, "thou palace of sight and sound, carrying in thy senses the morning and the night and the unfathomable galaxy; in thy brain the geometry of the city of God; in thy heart the bower of love and the realms of right and wrong."

If the individual open thus directly into the Absolute, it follows that there is something in each and all of us, even the lowliest, that ought not to consent to borrowing traditions and living at second hand. "If John was perfect, why are you and I alive?" Emerson writes; "As long as any man exists there is some need of him; let him fight for his own." This faith that in a life at first hand there is some-

24

thing sacred is perhaps the most characteristic note in Emerson's writings. The hottest
side of him is this non-conformist persuasion,
and if his temper could ever verge on common
irascibility, it would be by reason of the passionate character of his feelings on this point.
The world is still new and untried. In seeing
freshly, and not in hearing of what others
saw, shall a man find what truth is. "Each
one of us can bask in the great morning which
rises out of the Eastern Sea, and be himself
one of the children of the light." "Trust
thyself, every heart vibrates to that iron
string. There is a time in each man's education when he must arrive at the conviction
that imitation is suicide; when he must take
himself for better or worse as his portion; and
know that though the wide universe is full of
good, no kernel of nourishing corn can come
to him but through his toil bestowed on that
plot of ground which it was given him to till."

The matchless eloquence with which Emerson proclaimed the sovereignty of the living
individual electrified and emancipated his

generation, and this bugle-blast will doubtless be regarded by future critics as the soul of his message. The present man is the aboriginal reality, the Institution is derivative, and the past man is irrelevant and obliterate for present issues. "If anyone would lay an axe to your tree with a text from 1 John, v, 7, or a sentence from Saint Paul, say to him," Emerson wrote, "'My tree is Yggdrasil, the tree of life.' Let him know by your security that your conviction is clear and sufficient, and, if he were Paul himself, that you also are here and with your Creator." "Cleave ever to God," he insisted, "against the name of God;" — and so, in spite of the intensely religious character of his total thought, when he began his career it seemed to many of his brethren in the clerical profession that he was little more than an iconoclast and desecrator.

Emerson's belief that the individual must in reason be adequate to the vocation for which the Spirit of the world has called him into being, is the source of those sublime pages, hearteners and sustainers of our youth, in

which he urges his hearers to be incorruptibly
true to their own private conscience. Nothing
can harm the man who rests in his appointed
place and character. Such a man is invul-
nerable; he balances the universe, balances
it as much by keeping small when he is small,
as by being great and spreading when he is
great. "I love and honor Epaminondas,"
said Emerson, "but I do not wish to be
Epaminondas. I hold it more just to love the
world of this hour than the world of his hour.
Nor can you, if I am true, excite me to the
least uneasiness by saying, ' He acted and thou
sittest still.' I see action to be good when
the need is, and sitting still to be also good.
Epaminondas, if he was the man I take him
for, would have sat still with joy and peace,
if his lot had been mine. Heaven is large, and
affords space for all modes of love and fortitude." "The fact that I am here certainly
shows me that the Soul has need of an organ
here, and shall I not assume the post?"

The vanity of all superserviceableness and
pretence was never more happily set forth

than by Emerson in the many passages in which he develops this aspect of his philosophy. Character infallibly proclaims itself. "Hide your thoughts! — hide the sun and moon. They publish themselves to the universe. They will speak through you though you were dumb. They will flow out of your actions, your manners and your face. . . . Don't say things: What you are stands over you the while and thunders so that I cannot say what you say to the contrary. . . . What a man *is* engraves itself upon him in letters of light. Concealment avails him nothing, boasting nothing. There is confession in the glances of our eyes; in our smiles; in salutations; and the grasp of hands. His sin bedaubs him, mars all his good impression. Men know not why they do not trust him, but they do not trust him. His vice glasses the eye, casts lines of mean expression in the cheek, pinches the nose, sets the mark of the beast upon the back of the head, and writes, O fool! fool! on the forehead of a king. If you would not be known to do a thing, never do it; a man may play the fool in the drifts of a desert, but every grain of sand shall seem to see. — How can a man be concealed? How can he be concealed?"

On the other hand, never was a sincere word or a sincere thought utterly lost. "Never a magnanimity fell to the ground but there is some heart to greet and accept it unexpectedly. . . . The hero fears not that if he withstood the avowal of a just and brave act, it will go unwitnessed and unloved. One knows it, — himself, — and is pledged by it to sweetness of peace and to nobleness of aim, which will prove in the end a better proclamation than the relating of the incident."

The same indefeasible right to be exactly what one is, provided one only be authentic, spreads itself, in Emerson's way of thinking, from persons to things and to times and places. No date, no position is insignificant, if the life that fills it out be only genuine:—

"In solitude, in a remote village, the ardent youth loiters and mourns. With inflamed eye, in this sleeping wilderness, he has read the story of the Emperor, Charles the Fifth, un-until his fancy has brought home to the sur-rounding woods the faint roar of cannonades in the Milanese, and marches in Germany. He is curious concerning that man's day. What filled it? The crowded orders, the stern decisions, the foreign despatches, the Castilian etiquette? The soul answers — Behold his day here! In the sighing of these woods, in the quiet of these gray fields, in the cool breeze that sings out of these northern moun-tains; in the workmen, the boys, the maidens you meet, — in the hopes of the morning, the *ennui* of noon, and sauntering of the after-noon; in the disquieting comparisons; in the regrets at want of vigor; in the great idea and the puny execution, — behold Charles the Fifth's day; another, yet the same; behold Chatham's, Hampden's, Bayard's, Alfred's, Scipio's, Pericles's day, — day of all that are born of women. The difference of circum-stance is merely costume. I am tasting the self-same life, — its sweetness, its greatness, its pain, which I so admire in other men. Do not foolishly ask of the inscrutable, obliterated past what it cannot tell, — the details of that nature, of that day, called Byron or Burke; — but ask it of the enveloping Now. . . . Be lord of a day, and you can put up your history books."

"The deep to-day which all men scorn" receives thus from Emerson superb revindication. "Other world! there is no other world." All God's life opens into the individual particular, and here and now, or nowhere, is reality. "The present hour is the decisive hour, and every day is doomsday."

Such a conviction that Divinity is everywhere may easily make of one an optimist of the sentimental type that refuses to speak ill of anything. Emerson's drastic perception of differences kept him at the opposite pole from this weakness. After you have seen men a few times, he could say, you find most of them as alike as their barns and pantries, and soon as musty and as dreary. Never was such a fastidious lover of significance and distinction, and never an eye so keen for their discovery.

His optimism had nothing in common with
that indiscriminate hurrahing for the Universe with which Walt Whitman has made us
familiar. For Emerson, the individual fact
and moment were indeed suffused with absolute radiance, but it was upon a condition that
saved the situation — they must be worthy
specimens, — sincere, authentic, archetypal;
they must have made connection with what
he calls the Moral Sentiment, they must in
some way act as symbolic mouthpieces of the
Universe's meaning. To know just which thing
does act in this way, and which thing fails
to make the true connection, is the secret
(somewhat incommunicable, it must be confessed) of seership, and doubtless we must not
expect of the seer too rigorous a consistency.
Emerson himself was a real seer. He could
perceive the full squalor of the individual fact,
but he could also see the transfiguration. He
might easily have found himself saying of
some present-day agitator against our Phil-
ippine conquest what he said of this or that re-
former of his own time. He might have called

him, as a private person, a tedious bore and canter. But he would infallibly have added what he then added: "It is strange and horrible to say this, for I feel that under him and his partiality and exclusiveness is the earth and the sea, and all that in them is, and the axis round which the Universe revolves passes through his body where he stands."

Be it how it may, then, this is Emerson's revelation: — The point of any pen can be an epitome of reality; the commonest person's act, if genuinely actuated, can lay hold on eternity. This vision is the head-spring of all his outpourings; and it is for this truth, given to no previous literary artist to express in such penetratingly persuasive tones, that posterity will reckon him a prophet, and, perhaps neglecting other pages, piously turn to those that convey this message. His life was one long conversation with the invisible divine, expressing itself through individuals and particulars: — "So nigh is grandeur to our dust, so near is God to man!"

I spoke of how shrunken the wraith, how

thin the echo, of men is after they are departed. Emerson's wraith comes to me now as if it were but the very voice of this victorious argument. His words to this effect are certain to be quoted and extracted more and more as time goes on, and to take their place among the Scriptures of humanity. "'Gainst death and all oblivious enmity, shall you pace forth," beloved Master. As long as our English language lasts men's hearts will be cheered and their souls strengthened and liberated by the noble and musical pages with which you have enriched it.

III

ROBERT GOULD SHAW

III

ROBERT GOULD SHAW[1]

Your Excellency, your Honor, Soldiers, and Friends: In these unveiling exercises the duty falls to me of expressing in simple words some of the feelings which have actuated the givers of St. Gaudens' noble work of bronze, and of briefly recalling the history of Robert Shaw and of his regiment to the memory of this possibly too forgetful generation.

The men who do brave deeds are usually unconscious of their picturesqueness. For two nights previous to the assault upon Fort Wagner, the Fifty-fourth Massachusetts Regiment had been afoot, making forced marches in the rain; and on the day of the battle the men had had no food since early morning. As they lay there in the evening twilight, hungry and wet, against the cold sands of Morris

[1] Oration at the Exercises in the Boston Music Hall, May 31, 1897, upon the Unveiling of the Shaw Monument.

Island, with the sea-fog drifting over them, their eyes fixed on the huge bulk of the fortress looming darkly three-quarters of a mile ahead against the sky, and their hearts beating in expectation of the word that was to bring them to their feet and launch them on their desperate charge, neither officers nor men could have been in any holiday mood of contemplation. Many and different must have been the thoughts that came and went in them during that hour of bodeful reverie; but however free the flights of fancy of some of them may have been, it is improbable that any one who lay there had so wild and whirling an imagination as to foresee in prophetic vision this morning of a future May, when we, the people of a richer and more splendid Boston, with mayor and governor, and troops from other States, and every circumstance of ceremony, should meet together to celebrate their conduct on that evening, and do their memory this conspicuous honor.

How, indeed, comes it that out of all the great engagements of the war, engagements in many of which the troops of Massachusetts had borne the most distinguished part, this officer, only a young colonel, this regiment of black men and its maiden battle, — a battle, moreover, which was lost, — should be picked out for such unusual commemoration?

The historic significance of an event is measured neither by its material magnitude, nor by its immediate success. Thermopylæ was a defeat; but to the Greek imagination, Leonidas and his few Spartans stood for the whole worth of Grecian life. Bunker Hill was a defeat; but for our people, the fight over that breastwork has always seemed to show as well as any victory that our forefathers were men of a temper not to be finally overcome. And so here. The war for our Union, with all the constitutional questions which it settled, and all the military lessons which it gathered in, has throughout its dilatory length but one meaning in the eye of history. And nowhere was that meaning better symbolized and embodied than in the constitution of this first Northern negro regiment.

Look at the monument and read the story; — see the mingling of elements which the sculptor's genius has brought so vividly before the eye. There on foot go the dark outcasts, so true to nature that one can almost hear them breathing as they march. State after State by its laws had denied them to be human persons. The Southern leaders in congressional debates, insolent in their security, loved most to designate them by the contemptuous collective epithet of "this peculiar kind of property." There they march, warm-blooded champions of a better day for man. There on horseback, among them, in his very habit as he lived, sits the blue-eyed child of fortune, upon whose happy youth every divinity had smiled. Onward they move together, a single resolution kindled in their eyes, and animating their otherwise so different frames. The bronze that makes their memory eternal betrays the very soul and secret of those awful years.

Since the 'thirties the slavery question had been the only question, and by the end of the 'fifties our land lay sick and shaking with it like a traveller who has thrown himself down at night beside a pestilential swamp, and in the morning finds the fever through the marrow of his bones. "Only muzzle the Abolition fanatics," said the South, "and all will be well again!" But the Abolitionists would not be muzzled, — they were the voice of the world's conscience, they were a part of destiny. Weak as they were, they drove the South to madness. "Every step she takes in her blindness," said Wendell Phillips, "is one more step towards ruin." And when South Carolina took the final step in battering down Fort Sumter, it was the fanatics of slavery themselves who called upon their idolized institution ruin swift and complete. What law and reason were unable to accomplish, had now to be done by that uncertain and dreadful dispenser of God's judgments, War — War, with its abominably casual, inaccurate methods, destroying good and bad together, but at last able to hew a way out of intolerable situations, when through man's

41

delusion of perversity every better way is blocked.

Our great western republic had from its origin been a singular anomaly. A land of freedom, boastfully so-called, with human slavery enthroned at the heart of it, and at last dictating terms of unconditional surrender to every other organ of its life, what was it but a thing of falsehood and horrible self-contradiction? For three-quarters of a century it had nevertheless endured, kept together by policy, compromise, and concession. But at the last that republic was torn in two; and truth was to be possible under the flag. Truth, thank God, truth! even though for the moment it must be truth written in hell-fire.

And this, fellow-citizens, is why, after the great generals have had their monuments, and long after the abstract soldier's-monuments have been reared on every village green, we have chosen to take Robert Shaw and his regiment as the subjects of the first soldier's-monument to be raised to a particular set of comparatively undistinguished men. The very lack of external complication in the history of these soldiers is what makes them represent with such typical purity the profounder meaning of the Union cause.

Our nation had been founded in what we may call our American religion, baptized and reared in the faith that a man requires no master to take care of him, and that common people can work out their salvation well enough together if left free to try. But the founders had not dared to touch the great intractable exception; and slavery had wrought until at last the only alternative for the nation was to fight or die. What Shaw and his comrades stand for and show us is that in such an emergency Americans of all complexions and conditions can go forth like brothers, and meet death cheerfully if need be, in order that this religion of our native land shall not become a failure on earth.

We of this Commonwealth believe in that religion; and it is not at all because Robert Shaw was an exceptional genius, but simply because he was faithful to it as we all may hope to be faithful in our measure when the times demand, that we wish his beautiful image to stand here for all time, an inciter to similarly unselfish public deeds.

Shaw thought but little of himself, yet he had a personal charm which, as we look back on him, makes us repeat: "None knew thee but to love thee, none named thee but to praise." This grace of nature was united in him in the happiest way with a filial heart, a cheerful will, and a judgment that was true and fair. And when the war came, and great things were doing of the kind that he could help in, he went as a matter of course to the front. What country under heaven has not thousands of such youths to rejoice in, youths on whom the safety of the human race depends? Whether or not they leave memorials behind them, whether their names are writ in water or in marble, depends mostly on the opportunities which the accidents of history throw into their path. Shaw recognized the vital opportunity: he saw that the time had come when the colored people must put the country in their debt.

Colonel Lee has just told us something about the obstacles with which this idea had to contend. For a large party of us this was still exclusively a white man's war; and should colored troops be tried and not succeed, confusion would grow worse confounded. Shaw was a captain in the Massachusetts Second, when Governor Andrew invited him to take the lead in the experiment. He was very modest, and doubted, for a moment, his own capacity for so responsible a post. We may also imagine human motives whispering other doubts. Shaw loved the Second Regiment, illustrious already, and was sure of promotion where he stood. In this new negro-soldier venture, loneliness was certain, ridicule inevitable, failure possible; and Shaw was only twenty-five; and, although he had stood among the bullets at Cedar Mountain and Antietam, he had till then been walking socially on the sunny side of life. But whatever doubts may have beset him, they were over in a day, for he inclined naturally toward difficult resolves. He accepted the proffered

45

command, and from that moment lived but for one object, to establish the honor of the Massachusetts Fifty-fourth.

I have had the privilege of reading his letters to his family from the day of April when, as a private in the New York Seventh, he obeyed the President's first call. Some day they must be published, for they form a veritable poem for serenity and simplicity of tone. He took to camp life as if it were his native element, and (like so many of our young soldiers) he was at first all eagerness to make arms his permanent profession. Drilling and disciplining; interminable marching and counter-marching, and picket-duty on the Upper Potomac as lieutenant in our Second Regiment, to which post he had soon been promoted; pride at the discipline attained by the Second, and horror at the bad discipline of other regiments; these are the staple matter of earlier letters, and last for many months. These, and occasional more recreative incidents, visits to Virginian houses, the reading of books like Napier's "Peninsular War," or the "Idylls of the

King," Thanksgiving feats, and races among officers, that helped the weary weeks to glide away. Then the bloodier business opens, and the plot thickens till the end is reached. From first to last there is not a rancorous word against the enemy, — often quite the reverse, — and amid all the scenes of hardship, death, and devastation that his pen soon has to write of, there is unfailing cheerfulness and even a sort of innermost peace.

After he left it, Robert Shaw's heart still clung to the fortunes of the Second. Months later when, in South Carolina with the Fifty-fourth, he writes to his young wife: "I should have been major of the Second now if I had remained there and lived through the battles. As regards my own pleasure, I had rather have that place than any other in the army. It would have been fine to go home a field officer in that regiment! Poor fellows, how they have been slaughtered!"

Meanwhile he had well taught his new command how to do their duty; for only three days after he wrote this he led them up the parapet of Fort Wagner, where he and nearly half of them were left upon the ground.

Robert Shaw quickly inspired others with his own love of discipline. There was something almost pathetic in the earnestness with which both the officers and men of the Fifty-fourth embraced their mission of showing that a black regiment could excel in every virtue known to man. They had good success, and the Fifty-fourth became a model in all possible respects. Almost the only trace of bitterness in Shaw's whole correspondence is over an incident in which he thought his men had been morally disgraced. It had become their duty, immediately after their arrival at the seat of war, to participate, in obedience to fanatical orders from the head of the department, in the sack and burning of the inoffensive little town of Darien on the Georgia coast. "I fear," he writes to his wife, "that such actions will hurt the reputation of black troops and of those connected with them. For myself I have gone through the war so far without dishonor, and I do not like to degen-

erate into a plunderer and a robber, — and
the same applies to every officer in my regiment. After going through the hard campaigning and the hard fighting in Virginia,
this makes me very much ashamed. There
are two courses only for me to pursue: to
obey orders and say nothing; or to refuse to
go upon any more such expeditions, and be put
under arrest and probably court-martialled,
which is a very serious thing." Fortunately
for Shaw, the general in command of that
department was almost immediately relieved.

Four weeks of camp life and discipline on
the Sea Islands, and the regiment had its
baptism of fire. A small affair, but it proved
the men to be staunch. Shaw again writes to
his wife: "You don't know what a fortunate
day this has been for me and for us all, ex-
cepting some poor fellows who were killed and
wounded. We have fought at last alongside
of white troops. Two hundred of my men on
picket this morning were attacked by five regiments of infantry, some cavalry, and a battery
of artillery. The Tenth Connecticut were on

their left, and say they would have had a bad time if the Fifty-fourth men had not stood so well. The whole division was under arms in fifteen minutes, and after coming up close in front of us, the enemy, finding us so strong, fell back. . . . General Terry sent me word he was highly gratified with the behavior of our men, and the officers and privates of other regiments praise us very much. All this is very gratifying to us personally, and a fine thing for the colored troops. I know this will give you pleasure for it wipes out the remembrance of the Darien affair, which you could not but grieve over, though we were innocent participators."

The adjutant of the Fifty-fourth, who made report of this skirmish to General Terry, well expresses the feelings of loneliness that still prevailed in that command: —

"The general's favorite regiment," writes the adjutant,[1] "the Twenty-fourth Massachu-

[1] G. W. James: "The Assault upon Fort Wagner," in *War Papers read before the Commandery of the State of Wisconsin, Military Order of the Loyal Legion of the United States.* Milwaukee, 1891.

setts Infantry, one of the best that had so far
faced the rebel foe, largely officered by Boston
men, was surrounding his headquarters. It
had been a living breathing suspicion with us
— perhaps not altogether justly — that all
white troops abhorred our presence in the
army, and that the Twenty-fourth would
rather hear of us in some remote corner of the
Confederacy than tolerate us in advance of
any battle in which they themselves were to
act as reserves or lookers-on. Can you not
then readily imagine the pleasure which I
felt as I alighted from my horse before General
Terry and his staff — I was going to say his
unfriendly staff, but of this I am not sure — to
report to him, with Colonel Shaw's compli-
ments, that we had repulsed the enemy without the loss of a single inch of ground. General
Terry bade me mount again and tell Colonel
Shaw that he was proud of the conduct of his
men, and that he must still hold the ground
against any future sortie of the enemy. You
can even now share with me the sensation of
that moment of soldierly satisfaction."

The next night but one after this episode was spent by the Fifty-fourth in disembarking on Morris Island in the rain, and at noon Colonel Shaw was able to report their arrival to General Strong, to whose brigade he was assigned. A terrific bombardment was playing on Fort Wagner, then the most formidable earthwork ever built, and the general, knowing Shaw's desire to place his men beside white troops, said to him: "Colonel, Fort Wagner is to be stormed this evening, and you may lead the column, if you say Yes. Your men, I know, are worn out, but do as you choose." Shaw's face brightened. "Before answering the general, he instantly turned to me," writes the adjutant, who reports the interview, "and said, 'Tell Colonel Hallowell to bring up the Fifty-fourth immediately.'"

This was done, and just before nightfall the attack was made. Shaw was serious, for he knew the assault was desperate, and had a premonition of his end. Walking up and down in front of the regiment, he briefly exhorted them to prove that they were men. Then he gave the order: "Move in quick time till within a hundred yards, then double quick and charge. Forward!" and the Fifty-fourth advanced to the storming, its colonel and colors at its head.

On over the sand, through a narrow defile which broke up the formation, double quick over the chevaux de frise, into the ditch and over it, as best they could, and up the rampart with Fort Sumter, which had seen them, playing on them, and Fort Wagner, now one mighty mound of fire, tearing out their lives. Shaw led from first to last. Gaining successfully the parapet, he stood there for a moment with uplifted sword, shouting, "Forward, Fifty-fourth!" and then fell headlong, with a bullet through his heart. The battle raged for nigh two hours. Regiment after regiment, following upon the Fifty-fourth, hurled themselves upon its ramparts, but Fort Wagner was nobly defended, and for that night stood safe. The Fifty-fourth withdrew after two-thirds of its officers and five-twelfths or nearly half its men had been shot down or bayoneted within the fortress or before its walls. It was good behavior for a regiment, no one of whose soldiers had had a musket in his hands more than eighteen weeks, and which had seen the enemy for the first time only two days before.

"The negroes fought gallantly," wrote a Confederate officer, "and were headed by as brave a colonel as ever lived."

As for the colonel, not a drum was heard nor a funeral note, not a soldier discharged his farewell shot, when the Confederates buried him, the morning after the engagement. His body, half stripped of its clothing, and the corpses of his dauntless negroes were flung into one common trench together, and the sand was shovelled over them, without a stake or stone to signalize the spot. In death as in life, then, the Fifty-fourth bore witness to the brotherhood of man. The lover of heroic history could wish for no more fitting sepulchre for Shaw's magnanimous young heart. There let his body rest, united with the forms of his brave nameless comrades. There let the breezes of the Atlantic sigh, and its gales roar their requiem, while this bronze effigy and these inscriptions keep their fame alive long after you and I and all who meet here are forgotten.

How soon, indeed, are human things forgotten! As we meet here this morning, the Southern sun is shining on their place of burial, and the waves sparkling and the sea-gulls circling around Fort Wagner's ancient site. But the great earthworks and their thundering cannon, the commanders and their followers, the wild assault and repulse that for a brief space made night hideous on that far-off evening, have all sunk into the blue gulf of the past, and for the majority of this generation are hardly more than an abstract name, a picture, a tale that is told. Only when some yellow-bleached photograph of a soldier of the 'sixties comes into our hands, with that odd and vivid look of individuality due to the moment when it was taken, do we realize the concreteness of that by-gone history, and feel how interminable to the actors in them were those leaden-footed hours and years. The photographs themselves erelong will fade utterly, and books of history and monuments like this alone will tell the tale. The great war for the Union will be like the siege of Troy; it will have taken its place· amongst all other "old, unhappy, far-off things and battles long ago."

In all such events two things must be distinguished — the moral service of them from the fortitude which they display. War has been much praised and celebrated among us of late as a school of manly virtue; but it is easy to exaggerate upon this point. Ages ago, war was the gory cradle of mankind, the grim-featured nurse that alone could train our savage progenitors into some semblance of social virtue, teach them to be faithful one to another, and force them to sink their selfishness in wider tribal ends. War still excels in this prerogative; and whether it be paid in years of service, in treasure, or in life-blood, the war tax is still the only tax that men ungrudgingly will pay. How could it be otherwise, when the survivors of one successful massacre after another are the beings from whose loins we and all our contemporary races spring? Man is once for all a fighting animal; centuries of peaceful history could not breed the battle-instinct out of us; and our pugnacity is the virtue least in need of reinforcement by reflection, least in need of orator's or poet's help.

What we really need the poet's and orator's help to keep alive in us is not, then, the common and gregarious courage which Robert Shaw showed when he marched with you, men of the Seventh Regiment. It is that more lonely courage which he showed when he dropped his warm commission in the glorious Second to head your dubious fortunes, negroes of the Fifty-fourth. That lonely kind of courage (civic courage as we call it in times of peace) is the kind of valor to which the monuments of nations should most of all be reared, for the survival of the fittest has not bred it into the bone of human beings as it has bred military valor; and of five hundred of us who could storm a battery side by side with others, perhaps not one would be found ready to risk his wordly fortunes all alone in resisting an enthroned abuse. The deadliest enemies of nations are not their foreign foes; they always dwell within their borders. And from these internal enemies civilization is always in need of being saved. The nation blest above all nations is she in whom the civic genius of the people does the saving day by day, by acts without external picturesqueness; by speaking, writing, voting reasonably; by smiting corruption swiftly; by good temper between parties; by the people knowing true men when they see them, and preferring them as leaders to rabid partisans or empty quacks. Such nations have no need of wars to save them. Their accounts with righteousness are always even; and God's judgments do not have to overtake them fitfully in bloody spasms and convulsions of the race.

The lesson that our war ought most of all to teach us is the lesson that evils must be checked in time, before they grow so great. The Almighty cannot love such long-postponed accounts, or such tremendous settlements. And surely He hates all settlements that do such quantities of incidental devils' work. Our present situation, with its rancors and delusions, what is it but the direct outcome of the added powers of government, the corruptions and inflations of the war? Every war leaves such miserable legacies, fatal seeds of future war and revolution, unless the civic virtues of the people save the State in time.

Robert Shaw had both kinds of virtue. As he then led his regiment against Fort Wagner, so surely would he now be leading us against all lesser powers of darkness, had his sweet young life been spared. You think of many as I speak of one. For, North and South, how many lives as sweet, unmonumented for the most part, commemorated solely in the hearts of mourning mothers, widowed brides, or friends did the inexorable war mow down! Instead of the full years of natural service from so many of her children, our country counts but their poor memories, "the tender grace of a day that is dead," lingering like echoes of past music on the vacant air.

But so and so only was it written that she should grow sound again. From that fatal earlier unsoundness those lives have brought for North and South together permanent release. The warfare is accomplished; the iniquity is pardoned. No future problem can be like that problem. No task laid on our children can compare in difficulty with the task with which their fathers had to deal. Yet as we face the future, tasks enough await us. The republic to which Robert Shaw and a quarter of a million like him were faithful unto death is no republic that can live at ease hereafter on the interest of what they have won. Democracy is still upon its trial. The civic genius of our people is its only bulwark, and neither laws nor monuments, neither battleships nor public libraries, nor great newspapers nor booming stocks; neither mechanical invention nor political adroitness, nor churches nor universities nor civil service examinations can save us from degeneration if the inner mystery be lost. That mystery, at once the secret and the glory of our English-speaking race, consists in nothing but two common habits, two inveterate habits carried into public life, — habits so homely that they lend themselves to no rhetorical expression, yet habits more precious, perhaps, than any that the human race has gained. They can never be too often pointed out or praised. One of them is the habit of trained and disciplined good temper towards the opposite party when it fairly wins its innings. It was by breaking away from this habit that the Slave States nearly wrecked our Nation. The other is that of fierce and merciless resentment toward every man or set of men who break the public peace. By holding to this habit the free States saved her life.

O my countrymen, Southern and Northern, brothers hereafter, masters, slaves, and enemies no more, let us see to it that both of those heirlooms are preserved. So may our ransomed country, like the city of the promise, lie forever foursquare under Heaven, and the ways of all the nations be lit up by its light.

IV
FRANCIS BOOTT

IV

FRANCIS BOOTT[1]

How often does it happen here in New England that we come away from a funeral with a feeling that the service has been insufficient. If it be purely ritual, the individuality of the departed friend seems to play too small a part in it. If the minister conducts it in his own fashion, it is apt to be too thin and monotonous, and if he were not an intimate friend, too remote and official. We miss direct discourse of simple human affection about the person, which we find so often in those lay speeches at the grave of which in France they set us nowadays so many good examples. In the case of the friend whose memory brings us together on the present occasion, it was easy to organize this supplementary service. Not everyone leaves musical compositions of his own to fill

[1] An address delivered at the Memorial Service to Francis Boott in the Harvard Chapel, Sunday, May 8, 1904. Printed in 38 *Harvard Monthly*, 125.

the hour with. And if we may believe that spirits can know aught of what transpires in the world which they have forsaken, it must please us all to think how dear old Francis Boott's shade must now be touched at seeing in the Chapel of this university to which his feelings clung so loyally, his music and his life at last become the subjects of cordial and admiring recognition and commemorated by so many of his neighbors. I can imagine nothing at any rate of which the foreknowledge could have given him deeper satisfaction. Shy and sensitive, craving praise as every normal human being craves it, yet getting little, he had, I think, a certain consciousness of living in the shadow. I greatly doubt whether his daydreams ever went so far as to let him imagine a service like this. Such a cordial and spontaneous outgoing towards him on our part would surprise as much as it would delight him.

His life was private in the strongest sense of the term. His contributions to literature were all anonymous, book-reviews chiefly, or letters and paragraphs in the New York Nation on musical or literary topics. Good as was their quality, and witty as was their form, — his only independent volume was an almost incredibly witty little book of charades in verse — they were too slight in bulk for commemoration; and it was only as a musical composer that he touched on any really public function. With so many of his compositions sounding in your ears, it would be out of place, even were I qualified, to attempt to characterize Mr. Boott's musical genius. Let it speak for itself. I prefer to speak of the man and friend whom we knew and whom so many of us loved so dearly.

One of the usual classifications of men is into those of expansive and those of conservative temper. The word conservative commonly suggests a dose of religious and political prejudice, and a fondness for traditional opinions. Mr. Boott was a liberal in politics and theology; and all his opinions were self-made, and as often as not at variance with every tradition. Yet in a wider sense he was profoundly conservative.

He respected bounds of ordinance, and emphasized the fact of limits. He knew well his own limits. The knowledge of them was in fact one of the things he lived by. To judge of abstract philosophy, of sculpture and painting, of certain lines of literary art, he admitted, was not of his competency. But within the sphere where he thought he had a right to judge, he parted his likes from his dislikes and preserved his preferences with a pathetic steadfastness. He was faithful in age to the lights that lit his youth, and obeyed at eve the voice obeyed at prime, with a consistency most unusual. Elsewhere the opinions of others might perplex him, but he laughed and let them live. Within his own appropriated sphere he was too scrupulous a lover of the truth not to essay to correct them, when he thought them erroneous. A certain appearance comes in here of a self-contradictory character, for Mr. Boott was primarily modest and sensitive, and all his interests and pre-occupations were with life's refinements and delicacies. Yet one's mind always pictured him as a rugged sort of person,

opposing successful resistance to all influences
that might seek to change his habits either of
feeling or of action. His admirable health,
his sober life, his regular walk twice a day,
whatever might be the weather, his invariable evenness of mood and opinion, so that,
when you once knew his range, he never dis-
appointed you — all this was at variance with
popular notions of the artistic temperament.
He was indeed, a man of reason, no romancer,
sentimentalist or dreamer, in spite of the fact
that his main interests were with the muses.
He was exact and accurate; affectionate, indeed, and sociable, but neither gregarious nor
demonstrative; and such words as "honest,"
"sturdy," "faithful," are the adjectives first
to rise when one thinks of him. A friend said
to me soon after his death: "I seem still to see
Mr. Boott, with his two feet planted on the
ground, and his cane in front of him, making
of himself a sort of tripod of honesty and
veracity."

Old age changes men in different ways.
Some it softens; some it hardens; some it de-

generates; some it alters. Our old friend Boott was identical in spiritual essence all his life, and the effect of his growing old was not to alter, but only to make the same man mellower, more tolerant, more lovable. Sadder he was, I think, for his life had grown pretty lonely; but he was a stoic and he never complained either of losses or of years, and that contagious laugh of his at any and every pretext for laughter rang as free and true upon his deathbed as at any previous time of his existence.

Born in 1813, he had lived through three generations, and seen enormous social and public changes. When a carpenter has a surface to measure, he slides his rule along it, and over all its peculiarities. I sometimes think of Boott as such a standard rule against which the changing fashions of humanity of the last century might come to measurement. A character as healthy and definite as his, of whatsoever type it be, need only remain entirely true to itself for a sufficient number of years, while the outer conditions change, to grow into some-

thing like a common measure. Compared
with its repose and permanent fitness to continue, the changes of the generations seem
ephemeral and accidental. It remains the
standard, the rule, the term of comparison.
Mr. Boott's younger friends must often have
felt in his presence how much more vitally near
they were than they had supposed to the old
Boston long before the war, to the older Harvard, to the older Rome and Florence. To
grow old after his manner is of itself to grow
important.

I said that Mr. Boott was not demonstrative or sentimental. Tender-hearted he was
and faithful as few men are, in friendship.
He made new friends, and dear ones, in the
very last years of his life, and it is good to
think of him as having had that consolation.
The will in which he surprised so many persons by remembering them — "one of the
only purely beautiful wills I have ever read,"
said a lawyer, — showed how much he cared
at heart for many of us to whom he had rarely
made express professions of affection.

Good-by, then, old friend. We shall never-more meet the upright figure, the blue eye, the hearty laugh, upon these Cambridge streets. But in that wider world of being of which this little Cambridge world of ours forms so infinitesimal a part, we may be sure that all our spirits and their missions here will continue in some way to be represented, and that ancient human loves will never lose their own.

V

THOMAS DAVIDSON: A KNIGHT-ERRANT OF THE INTELLECTUAL LIFE.

V

THOMAS DAVIDSON: A KNIGHT-ERRANT OF THE INTELLECTUAL LIFE.[1]

I wish to pay my tribute to the memory of a Scottish-American friend of mine who died five years ago, a man of a character extraordinarily and intensely human, in spite of the fact that he was classed by obituary articles in England among the twelve most learned men of his time.

It would do no honor to Thomas Davidson's memory not to be frank about him. He handled people without gloves, himself, and one has no right to retouch his photograph until its features are softened into insipidity. He had defects and excesses which he wore upon his sleeve, so that everyone could see them. They made him many enemies, and if one liked quarrelling he was an easy man to

[1] First published in *McClure's Magazine* for May, 1905.

quarrel with. But his heart and mind held treasures of the rarest. He had a genius for friendship. Money, place, fashion, fame, and other vulgar idols of the tribe had no hold on his imagination. He led his own life absolutely, in whatever company he found himself, and the intense individualism which he taught by word and deed, is the lesson of which our generation is perhaps most in need.

All sorts of contrary adjectives come up as I think of him. To begin with, there was something physically rustic which suggested to the end his farm-boy origin. His voice was sweet and its Scottish cadences most musical, and the extraordinary sociability of his nature made friends for him as much among women as among men; he had, moreover, a sort of physical dignity; but neither in dress nor in manner did he ever grow quite "gentlemanly " or *Salonfähig* in the conventional and obliterated sense of the terms. He was too cordial and emphatic for that. His broad brow, his big chest, his bright blue eyes, his volubility in talk and laughter told a tale of vitality far

THOMAS DAVIDSON

beyond the common; but his fine and nervous
hands, and the vivacity of all his reactions
suggested a degree of sensibility that one
rarely finds conjoined with so robustly animal
a frame. The great peculiarity of Davidson
did indeed consist in this combination of the
acutest sensibilities with massive faculties of
thought and action, a combination which,
when the thought and actions are important,
gives to the world its greatest men.

Davidson's native mood was happy. He
took optimistic views of life and of his own
share in it. A sort of permanent satisfaction
radiated from his face; and this expression
of inward glory (which in reality was to a
large extent structural and not " expressive "
at all) was displeasing to many new acquaintances on whom it made an impression of too
much conceit. The impression of conceit was
not diminished in their eyes by the freedom
with which Davidson contradicted, corrected
and reprehended other people. A longer acquaintance invariably diminished the impression. But it must be confessed that T. D.

77

never was exactly humble-minded, and that the solidity of his self-consciousness withstood strains under which that of weaker men would have crumbled. The malady which finally killed him was one of the most exhausting to the nervous tone to which our flesh is subject, and it wore him out before it ended him. He told me of the paroxysms of motiveless nervous dread which used to beset him in the night-watches. Yet these never subdued his stalwartness, nor made him a " sick-soul " in the theological sense of that appelation. " God is afraid of me," was the phrase by which he described his well-being to me one morning when his night had been a good one, and he was feeling so cannibalistic that he thought he might get well.

There are men whose attitude is always that of seeking for truth, and men who on the contrary always believe that they have the root of it already in them. Davidson was of the latter class. Like his countrymen, Carlyle and Ruskin, he felt himself to be in the possession of something, whether articulate or as yet

inarticulated by himself, that authorized him
(and authorized him with uncommon open-
ness and frequency) to condemn the errors of
others. I think that to the last he never fully
extricated this philosophy. It was a tendency, a faith in a direction, which gave him
an active persuasion that other directions were
false, but of which the central insight never
got fully formulated, but remained in a state
which Frederic Myers would have called subliminal. He varied to a certain extent his
watchwords and his heroes. When I first knew
him all was Aristotle. Later all was Rosmini.
Later still Rosmini seemed forgotten. He
knew so many writers that he grew fond of
very various ones and had a strange tolerance
for systematizers and dogmatizers whom, as
the consistent individualist that he was, he
should have disliked. Hegel, it is true, he
detested; but he always spoke with reverence
of Kant. Of Mill and Spencer he had a low
opinion; and when I lent him Paulsen's Introduction to Philosophy (then just out), as an
example of a kind of eclectic thought that

seemed to be growing, and with which I largely sympathized, he returned it with richer expressions of disdain than often fell even from his lips: "It's the shabbiest, seediest pretence at a philosophy I ever dreamed of as possible. It's like a man dressed in a black coat so threadbare as to be all shiny. The most poverty-stricken, out-at-elbows thing I ever read. A perfect monument of seediness and shabbiness," etc.

The truth is that Davidson, brought up on the older classical traditions, never outgrew those habits of judging the world by purely æsthetic criteria which men fed on the sciences of nature are so willing to abandon. Even if a philosophy were true, he could easily fail to relish it unless it showed a certain formal nobility and dogmatic pretension to finality. But I must not describe him so much from my own professional point of view — it is as a vessel of life at large that one ought to keep him in remembrance.

He came to Boston from St. Louis, where he had been teaching, about the year 1873.

He was ruddy and radiant, and I soon saw much of him, though at first it was without the thoroughness of sympathy which we afterwards acquired and which made us overflow, on meeting after long absences, into such laughing greetings as: "Ha! you old thief! Ha! you old blackguard!" — pure "contrast-effects" of affection and familiarity passing beyond their bounds. At that time I saw most of him at a little philosophical club which used to meet every fortnight at his rooms in Temple Street in Boston. Of the other members, J. Elliot Cabot and C. C. Everett, are now dead — I will not name the survivors. We never worked out harmonious conclusions. Davidson used to crack the whip of Aristotle over us; and I remember that, whatever topic was formally appointed for the day, we invariably wound up with a quarrel about Space and Space-perception. The Club had existed before Davidson's advent. The previous year we had gone over a good part of Hegel's larger Logic, under the self-constituted leadership of two young business men from Illinois, who had become enthusiastic Hegelians and, knowing almost no German, had actually possessed themselves of a manuscript translation of the entire three volumes of Logic, made by an extraordinary Pomeranian immigrant, named Brockmeyer. These disciples were leaving business for the law and studying at the Harvard law-school; but they saw the whole universe through Hegelian spectacles, and a more admirable *homo unius libri* than one of them, with his three big folios of Hegelian manuscript, I have never had the good fortune to know.

I forget how Davidson was earning his subsistence at this time. He did some lecturing and private teaching, but I do not think they were great in amount. In the springs and summers he frequented the coast, and indulged in long swimming bouts and salt-water immersions, which seemed to agree with him greatly. His sociability was boundless, and his time seemed to belong to anyone who asked for it.

I soon conceived that such a man would be invaluable in Harvard University — a kind of

Socrates, a devotee of truth and lover of youth, ready to sit up to any hour, and drink beer and talk with anyone, lavish of learning and counsel, a contagious example of how lightly and humanly a burden of erudition might be borne upon a pair of shoulders. In faculty-business he might not run well in harness, but as an inspiration and ferment of character, as an example of the ranges of combination of scholarship with manhood that are possible, his influence on the students would be priceless.

I do not know whether this scheme of mine could under any circumstances have been carried out. In point of fact it was nipped in the bud by T. D. himself. A natural chair for him would have been Greek philosophy. Unfortunately, just at the decisive hour, he offended our Greek department by a savage onslaught on its methods, which, without taking anyone's counsel, he sent to the *Atlantic Monthly*, whose editor printed it. This, with his other unconventionalisms, made advocating his cause more difficult, and the university authorities, never, I believe, seriously thought of an appointment for him.

I believe that in this case, as in one or two others like it, which I might mention, Harvard University lost a great opportunity. Organization and method mean much, but contagious human characters mean more in a university, where a few undisciplinables like T. D. may be infinitely more precious than a faculty-full of orderly routinists. As to what Davidson might have become under the conventionalizing influences of an official position, it would be idle to speculate.

As things fell out, he became more and more unconventional and even developed a sort of antipathy to all regular academic life. It subdued individuality, he thought, and made for Philistinism. He earnestly dissuaded his young friend Bakewell from accepting a professorship; and I well remember one dark night in the Adirondacks, after a good dinner at a neighbor's, the eloquence with which, as we trudged down-hill to his own quarters with a lantern, he denounced me for the musty and

mouldy and generally ignoble academicism
of my character. Never before or since, I
fancy, has the air of the Adirondack wilderness vibrated more repugnantly to a vo-
cable than it did that night to the word
" academicism."

Yet Davidson himself was always essentially a teacher. He must give forth, inspire,
and have the young about him. After leaving Boston for Europe and Africa, founding
the Fellowship of the New Life in London and
New York (the present Fabian Society in
England is its offshoot), he hit upon the plan
which pleased him best of all when, in 1882 or
thereabouts, he bought a couple of hundred
acres on East Hill, which closes the beautiful
Keene Valley in the Adirondacks, on the north,
and founded there, at the foot of Hurricane
Mountain, his place "Glenmore" and its
"Summer School of the Culture Sciences."
Although the primeval forest has departed
from its immediate vicinity, the region is still
sylvan, the air is sweet and strong and almost
alpine in quality, and the mountain panorama

spread before one is superlative. Davidson showed a business faculty which I should hardly have expected from him, in organizing his settlement. He built a number of cottages, pretty in design and of the simplest construction, and disposed them well for effect. He turned a couple of farm buildings which were on the grounds into a lecturing place and a refectory; and there, arriving in early April and not leaving till late in November, he spent the happiest part of all his later years, surrounded during the summer months by colleagues, friends, and listeners to lectures, and in the spring and fall by a few independent women who were his faithful friends, and who had found East Hill a congenial residence.

Twice I went up with T. D. to open the place in April. I remember leaving his fireside one night with three ladies who were also early comers, and finding the thermometer at 8° Fahrenheit and a tremendous gale blowing the snow about us. Davidson loved these blustering vicissitudes of climate. In the early years the brook was never too cold for him to bathe in, and he spent days in rambling over the hills and up the glens and through the forest.

His own cottage was full of books whose use was free to all who visited the settlement. It stood high on a hill in a grove of silver-birches and looked upon the Western Mountains; and it always seemed to me an ideal dwelling for such a bachelor-scholar. Here in May and June he became almost one with the resurgent vegetation. Here, in October, he was a witness of the jewelled pageant of the dying foliage, and saw the hillsides reeking, as it were, and aflame with ruby and gold and emerald and topaz. One September day in 1900, at the " Kurhaus " at Nauheim, I took up a copy of the Paris *New York Herald*, and read in capitals: " Death of Professor Thomas Davidson." I had well known how ill he was, yet such was his vitality that the shock was wholly unexpected. I did not realize till that moment how much that free companionship with him every spring and autumn, surrounded by that beautiful nature, had signified to me, or how big a piece would be subtracted from my life by its cessation.

Davidson's capacity for imparting information seemed endless. There were few subjects, especially "humanistic" subjects, in which at some time or other he had not taken an interest; and as everything that had ever touched him was instantaneously in reach of his omnipotent memory, he easily became a living dictionary of reference. As such all his friends were wont to use him. He was, for example, never at a loss to supply a quotation. He loved poetry passionately, and the sympathetic voice with which he would recall page after page of it — English, French, German, or Italian — is a thing always to be remembered. But notwithstanding the instructive part he played in every conceivable conversation, he was never prolix, and he never "lectured."

From Davidson I learned what immunities a perfect memory bestows upon one. I never could discover when he amassed his learning, for he never seemed "occupied." The secret of it was that any odd time would do, for he never had to acquire a thing twice over. He avoided stated hours of work on principle. Reprehending (mildly) a certain chapter of my own on "Habit," he said that it was a fixed rule with him to form no regular habits. When he found himself in danger of settling into even a good one, he made a point of interrupting it. Habits and methods make a prisoner of a man, destroy his readiness, keep him from answering the call of the fresh moment. Individualist *à outrance*, Davidson felt that every hour was an unique entity, to whose claims one should lie open. Thus he was never abstracted or pre-occupied, but always seemed, when with you, as if you were the one person whom it was then right to attend to.

It was this individualistic religion that made T. D., democrat as he nevertheless was, so hostile to all socialisms and administrative panaceas. Life must be flexible. You ask for a free man, and these utopias give you an "in-terchangeable part," with a fixed number, in a rule-bound organism. The real thing to aim at is liberation of the inner interests. Give a man possession of a *soul*, and he will work out his own happiness under any set of conditions. Accordingly, when, in the penultimate year of his life, he proposed his night-school to a meeting of young East-Side workingmen in New York, he told them that he had no sympathy whatever with the griefs of "labor," that outward circumstances meant nothing in his eyes; that through their individual wills and intellects they could share, just as they were, in the highest spiritual life of humanity, and that he was there to help them severally to that privilege.

The enthusiasm with which they responded speaks volumes, both for his genius as a teacher and for the sanity of his position. A small posthumous book of articles by Davidson and of letters written from Glenmore to his class, just published, with an introduction by his disciple Professor Bakewell,[1] gives a full account of the experiment, and ought to stand

[1] "The Education of the Wage-Earners." Boston, Ginn & Company, 1904.

as a model and inspirer to similar attempts the world over. Davidson's idea of the universe was that of a republic of immortal spirits, the chief business of whom in their several grades of existence, should be to know and love and help one another. "Creeds are nothing, life is everything. . . . You can do far more by presenting to the world the example of noble social relations than by enumerating any set of principles. Know all you can, love all you can, do all you can — that is the whole duty of man. . . . Be friends, in the truest sense, each to the other. There is nothing in all the world like friendship, when it is deep and real. . . . The divine . . . is a republic of self-existent spirits, each seeking the realization of its ideas through love, through intimacy with all the rest, and finding its heaven in such intimacy."

We all say and think that we believe this sort of thing; but Davidson believed it really and actively, and that made all the difference. When the young wage-earners whom he addressed found that here was a man of measureless learning ready to give his soul to them, as if he had nothing else to do with it, life's ideal possibilities widened to their view. When he was taken from them, they founded in New York the Thomas Davidson Society, for study and neighborhood work, which will probably become perpetual, and of which his epistles from Glenmore will be the rule, and keep the standards set by him from degenerating — unless, indeed, the Society should some day grow too rich, of which there is no danger at present, and from which may Heaven long preserve it. In one of his letters to the Class, Davidson sums up the results of his own experience of life in twenty maxims, as follows:

1. Rely upon your own energies, and do not wait for, or depend on other people.

2. Cling with all your might to your own highest ideals, and do not be led astray by such vulgar aims as wealth, position, popularity. Be yourself.

3. Your worth consists in what you are, and not in what you have. What you are will show in what you do.

4. Never fret, repine, or envy. Do not make yourself unhappy by comparing your circumtancs with those of more fortunate people; but make the most of the opportunities you have. Employ profitably every moment.

5. Associate with the noblest people you can find; read the best books; live with the mighty. But learn to be happy alone.

6. Do not believe that all greatness and heroism are in the past. Learn to discover princes, prophets, heroes, and saints among the people about you. Be assured they are there.

7. Be on earth what good people hope to be in heaven.

8. Cultivate ideal friendships, and gather into an intimate circle all your acquaintances who are hungering for truth and right. Remember that heaven itself can be nothing but the intimacy of pure and noble souls.

9. Do not shrink from any useful or kindly act, however hard or repellent it may be. The worth of acts is measured by the spirit in which they are performed.

10. If the world despise you because you do not follow its ways, pay no heed to it. But be sure your way is right.

11. If a thousand plans fail, be not disheartened. As long as your purposes are right, *you* have not failed.

12. Examine yourself every night, and see whether you have progressed in knowledge, sympathy, and helpfulness during the day. Count every day a loss in which no progress has been made.

13. Seek enjoyment in energy, not in dalliance. Our worth is measured solely by what we do.

14. Let not your goodness be professional; let it be the simple, natural outcome of your character. Therefore cultivate character.

15. If you do wrong, say so, and make what atonement you can. That is true nobleness. Have no moral debts.

16. When in doubt how to act, ask yourself, What does nobility command? Be on good terms with yourself.

17. Look for no reward for goodness but goodness itself. Remember heaven and hell are utterly immoral institutions, if they are meant as reward and punishment.

18. Give whatever countenance and help you can to every movement and institution that is working for good. Be not sectarian.

19. Wear no placards, within or without. Be human fully.

20. Never be satisfied until you have understood the meaning of the world, and the purpose of our own life, and have reduced *your* world to a rational cosmos.

One of the "placards" Davidson tried hardest to keep his Society from wearing was that of "Socialism." Yet no one felt more deeply than he the evils of rapacious individual competition. Spontaneously and flexibly organized social settlements or communities, with individual leaders as their centres, seem to have been his ideal, each with its own religious or ethical elements of discipline. The present isolation of the family is too inhuman. The ideal type of future life, he thought, will be something like the monastery, with the family instead of the individual, for its unit.

Leveller upwards of men as Davidson was, upon the intellectual and moral level, he seemed wholly without that sort of religion which makes so many of our contemporary anarchists think that they ought to dip, at least, into some manual occupation, in order to share the common burden of humanity. I never saw T. D. work with his hands in any way. He accepted material services of all kinds without apology, as if he were a patrician, evidently feeling that if he played his own more intellectual part rightly, society could make no further claim upon him.

This confidence that the life of the spirit is the absolutely highest, made Davidson serene about his outward fortunes. Pecuniary worry would not tally with his program. He had a very small provision against a rainy day, but he did little to increase it. He used to write as many articles and give as many "lectures," "talks," or "readings" every winter as would suffice to pay the year's expenses, and thereafter he refused additional invitations, and repaired to Glenmore as early in the spring as possible. I could but admire the temper he showed when the principal building there was one night burned to ashes. There was no insurance on it, and it would cost a couple of thousand dollars to replace it. Excitable as

Davidson was about small contrarieties, he watched this fire without a syllable of impatience. *Plaie d'argent n'est pas mortelle*, he seemed to say, and if he felt sharp regrets, he disdained to express them.

No more did care about his literary reputation trouble him. In the ordinary greedy sense, he seemed quite free from ambition. During his last years he had prepared a large amount of material for that history of the interaction of Greek, Christian, Hebrew, and Arabic thought upon one another before the revival of learning, which was to be his *magnum opus*. It was a territory to which, in its totality, few living minds had access, and in which a certain proprietary feeling was natural. Knowing how short his life might be, I once asked him whether he felt no concern lest the work already done by him should be frustrate, from the lack of its necessary complement, in case he were suddenly cut off. His answer surprised me by its indifference. He would work as long as he lived, he said, but not allow himself to worry, and look serenely at whatever

97

might be the outcome. This seemed to me un-commonly high-minded. I think that David-son's conviction of immortality had much to do with such a superiority to accidents. On the surface, and towards small things, he was irritable enough, but the undertone of his character was remarkable for equanimity. He showed it in his final illness, of which the misery was really atrocious. There were no general complaints or lamentations about the personal situation or the arrest to his career. It was the human lot and he must even bear it; so he kept his mind upon objective matters.

But, as I said at the outset, the paramount thing in Davidson in my eyes was his capacity for friendship. His friends were innumerable — boys and girls and old boys and old girls, Pa-pists and Protestants, Jews and Gentiles, mar-ried and single; and he cared deeply for each one of them, admiring them often too extrava-gantly. What term can name those recurrent waves of delighted laughter that expressed his greeting, beginning from the moment he saw

you, and accompanying his words continuously, as if his pleasure in you were interminable? His hand too, stretched out when
yards away, so that a country neighbor said
it reached farther than any hand he ever met
with. The odd thing was that friendship in
Davidson seemed so little to interfere with
criticism. Persons with whom intercourse was
one long contradiction on his part, and who
appeared to annoy him to extermination, he
none the less loved tenderly, and enjoyed living with them. "He 's the most utterly selfish,
illiberal and narrow-hearted human being I
ever knew," I heard him once say of someone,
"and yet he's the dearest, nicest fellow living."
His enthusiastic belief in any young person
who gave a promise of genius was touching.
Naturally a man who is willing, as he was, to
be a prophet, always finds some women who
are willing to be disciples. I never heard of any
sentimental weakness in Davidson in this relation, save possibly in one case. They
warmed themselves at the fire of his soul, and
he told them truths without accommodation.

"You 're farther off from God than any woman I ever heard of." "Nay, if you believe in a protective tariff, you 're in hell already, though you may not know it." "You had a fine hysterical time last night, did n't you, when Miss B was brought up from the ravine with her dislocated shoulder." To Miss B he said: "I don't pity you. It served you right for being so ignorant as to go there at that hour." Seldom, strange to say, did the recipients of these deliverances seem to resent them.

What with Davidson's warmth of heart and sociability, I used to wonder at his never marrying. Two years before his death he told me the reason — an unhappy youthful love-affair in Scotland. Twice in later life, he said, temptation had come to him, and he had had to make his decision. When he had come to the point, he had felt each time that the tie with the dead girl was prohibitive. "When two persons have known each other as we did," he said, "neither can ever fully belong to a stranger. So it would n't do." "It would n't

100

do, it would n't do!" he repeated, as we lay on the hillside, in a tone so musically tender that it chimes in my ear now as I write down his confession. It can surely be no breach of confidence to publish it — it is too creditable to the profundity of Davidson's affections. As I knew him, he was one of the purest of human beings.

If one asks, now, what the *value* of Thomas Davidson was, what was the general significance of his life, apart from his particular books and articles, I have to say that it lay in the example he set to us all of how, even in the midst of this intensely worldly social system of ours, in which each human interest is organized so collectively and so commercially, a single man may still be a knight-errant of the intellectual life, and preserve full freedom in the midst of sociability. Extreme as was his need of friends, and faithful as he was to them, he yet lived mainly in reliance on his private inspiration. Asking no man's permission, bowing the knee to no tribal idol, renouncing the conventional channels of recognition, he

showed us how a life devoted to purely intellectual ends could be beautifully wholesome
outwardly, and overflow with inner contentment. Fortunately this type of man is recurrent, and from generation to generation, literary history preserves examples. But it is in-
frequent enough for few of us to have known
more than one example — I count myself
happy in knowing two and a half! The memory of Davidson will always strengthen my
faith in personal freedom and its spontaneities,
and make me less unqualifiedly respectful than
ever of "Civilization," with its herding and
branding, licensing and degree-giving, author-
izing and appointing, and in general regulating
and administering by system the lives of
human beings. Surely the individual, the
person in the singular number, is the more
fundamental phenomenon, and the social institution, of whatever grade, is but secondary
and ministerial. Many as are the interests
which social systems satisfy, always unsatisfied interests remain over, and among them
are interests to which system, as such, does

violence whenever it lays its hand upon us. The best Commonwealth will always be the one that most cherishes the men who represent the residual interests, the one that leaves the largest scope to their peculiarities.

VI

HERBERT SPENCER'S
AUTOBIOGRAPHY

VI

HERBERT SPENCER'S
AUTOBIOGRAPHY[1]

"God moves in a mysterious way his wonders to perform." If the greatest of all his
wonders be the human individual, the richness
with which the specimens thereof are diver-
sified, the limitless variety of outline, from
gothic to classic or flowing arabesque, the
contradictory nature of the filling, composed
of little and great, of comic, heroic, and pathetic elements blended inextricably, in personalities all of whom can *go*, and go successfully, must surely be reckoned the supreme
miracle of creative ingenuity. Rarely has
Nature performed an odder or more Dickens-
like feat than when she deliberately designed,
or accidentally stumbled into, the personality
of Herbert Spencer. Greatness and smallness

[1] Written upon the publication of Herbert Spencer's "Autobiography." Published in the *Atlantic
Monthly* for July, 1904.

surely never lived so closely in one skin together.

The opposite verdicts passed upon his work by his contemporaries bear witness to the extraordinary mingling of defects and merits in his mental character. Here are a few, juxtaposed: —

"A philosophic saw-mill." — "The most capacious and powerful thinker of all time."

"The ' Arry ' of philosophy." — "Aristotle and his master were not more beyond the pygmies who preceded them than he is beyond Aristotle."

"Herbert Spencer's chromo-philosophy." — "No other man that has walked the earth has so wrought and written himself into the life of the world."

"The touch of his mind takes the living flavor out of everything." — "He is as much above and beyond all the other great philosophers who have ever lived as the telegraph is beyond the carrier-pigeon, or the railway beyond the sedan chair."

"He has merely combined facts which we

knew before into a huge fantastic contradictory system, which hides its nakedness and emptiness partly under the veil of an imposing terminology, and partly in the primeval fog."
— "His contributions are of a depth, profundity, and magnitude which have no parallel in the history of mind. Taking but one — and one only — of his transcendent reaches of thought, — namely, that referring to the positive sense of the Unknown as the basis of religion, — it may unhesitatingly be affirmed that the analysis and synthesis by which he advances to the almost supernal grasp of this mighty truth give a sense of power and reach verging on the preternatural."

Can the two thick volumes of autobiography which Mr. Spencer leaves behind him explain such discrepant appreciations? Can we find revealed in them the higher synthesis which reconciles the contradictions? Partly they do explain, I think, and even justify, both kinds of judgment upon their author. But I confess that in the last resort I still feel baffled. In Spencer, as in every concrete individual,

109

there is a uniqueness that defies all formulation. We can feel the touch of it and recognize its taste, so to speak, relishing or disliking, as the case may be, but we can give no ultimate account of it, and we have in the end simply to admire the Creator.

Mr. Spencer's task, the unification of all knowledge into an articulate system, was more ambitious than anything attempted since St. Thomas or Descartes. Most thinkers have confined themselves either to generalities or to details, but Spencer addressed himself to everything. He dealt in logical, metaphysical, and ethical first principles, in cosmogony and geology, in physics, and chemistry after a fashion, in biology, psychology, sociology, politics, and æsthetics. Hardly any subject can be named which has not at least been touched on in some one of his many volumes. His erudition was prodigious. His civic conscience and his social courage both were admirable. His life was pure. He was devoted to truth and usefulness, and his character was wholly free from envy and malice

110

(though not from contempt), and from the perverse egoisms that so often go with greatness.

Surely, any one hearing this veracious enumeration would think that Spencer must have been a rich and exuberant human being. Such wide curiosities must have gone with the widest sympathies, and such a powerful harmony of character, whether it were a congenital gift, or were acquired by spiritual wrestling and eating bread with tears, must in any case have been a glorious spectacle for the beholder. Since Goethe, no such ideal human being can have been visible, walking our poor earth.

Yet when we turn to the "Autobiography," the self-confession which we find is this: An old-maidish personage, inhabiting boarding-houses, equable and lukewarm in all his tastes and passions, having no desultory curiosity, showing little interest in either books or people. A petty fault-finder and stickler for trifles, devoid in youth of any wide designs on life, fond only of the more mechanical side of things, yet drifting as it were involuntarily into

111

the possession of a world-formula which by dint of his extraordinary pertinacity he proceeded to apply to so many special cases that it made him a philosopher in spite of himself. He appears as modest enough, but with a curious vanity in some of his deficiencies, — his lack of desultory interests, for example, and his nonconformity to reigning customs. He gives a queer sense of having no emotional perspective, as if small things and large were on the same plane of vision, and equally commanded his attention. In spite of his professed dislike of monotony, one feels an awfully monotonous quality in him; and in spite of the fact that invalidism condemned him to avoid thinking, and to saunter and potter through large parts of every day, one finds no twilight region in his mind, and no capacity for dreaminess or passivity. All parts of it are filled with the same noonday glare, like a dry desert where every grain of sand shows singly, and there are no mysteries or shadows.

"Look on this picture and on that," and answer how they can be compatible.

For one thing, Mr. Spencer certainly writes himself *down* too much. He complains of a poor memory, of an idle disposition, of a general dislike for reading. Doubtless there have been more gifted men in all these respects. But when Spencer once buckled to a particular task, his memory, his industry, and his reading went beyond those of the most gifted. He had excessive sensibility to stimulation by a challenge, and he had preëminent pertinacity. When the notion of his philosophic system once grasped him, it seemed to possess itself of every effective fibre of his being. No faculty in him was left unemployed, — nor, on the other hand, was anything that his philosophy could contain left unstated. Roughly speaking, the task and the man absorbed each other without residuum.

Compare this type of mind with such an opposite type as Ruskin's, or even as J. S. Mill's, or Huxley's, and you realize its peculiarity. Behind the work of those others was a background of overflowing mental temptations. The men loom larger than all their publications, and leave an impression of unexpressed potentialities. Spencer tossed all his inexpressibilities into the Unknowable, and gladly turned his back on them forever. His books seem to have expressed all that there was to express in his character.

He is very frank about this himself. No *Sturm und Drang Periode*, no problematic stage of thought, where the burden of the much-to-be-straightened exceeds the powers of straightening.

When George Eliot uttered surprise at seeing no lines on his forehead, his reply was: —

"I suppose it is because I am never puzzled." — "It has never been my way," he continues, "to set before myself a problem and puzzle out an answer. The conclusions at which I have from time to time arrived, have not been arrived at as solutions of questions raised; but have been arrived at unawares — each as the ultimate outcome of a body of thought which slowly grew from a germ. Some direct observation, or some fact met with in reading, would dwell with me; apparently because I had a sense of its significance. . . . A week afterwards, possibly, the matter would be remembered; and with further thought about it, might occur a recognition of some wider application: new instances being aggregated with those already noted. Again, after an interval," etc., etc. "And thus, little by little, in unobtrusive ways, without conscious intention or appreciable effort, there would grow up a coherent and organized theory" (vol. i, page 464).

A sort of mill, this, wound up to grind in a certain way, and irresponsive otherwise.

"To apply day after day merely with the general idea of acquiring information, or of increasing ability, was not in me." "Anything like passive receptivity is foreign to my nature; and there results an unusually small tendency to be affected by others' thoughts. It seems as though the fabric of my conclusions had in all cases to be developed from within. Material which could be taken in and organized so as to form part of a coherent structure, there was always a readiness to receive. But ideas and sentiments of alien kinds, or unorganizable kinds, were, if not rejected, yet accepted with indifference, and soon dropped away." "It has always been out of the question for me to go on reading a book the fundamental principles of which I entirely dissent from. I take it for granted that if the fundamental principles are wrong the rest cannot be right; and thereupon cease reading — being, I suspect, rather glad of an excuse for doing so." "Systematic books of a political or ethical kind, written from points of view quite unlike my own, were either not consulted at all, or else they were glanced at and thereafter disregarded " (vol. i, pages 215, 277, 289, 350).

There is pride rather than compunction in these confessions. Spencer's mind was so narrowly systematized, that he was at last almost incapable of believing in the reality of alien ways of feeling. The invariable arrogance of his replies to criticisms shows his absolute self-confidence. Every opinion in the world had to be articulately right or articulately wrong, — so proved by some principle or other of his infallible system.

He confesses freely his own inflexibility and censoriousness. His account of his father makes one believe in the fatality of heredity. Born of old nonconformist stock, the elder Spencer was a man of absolute punctuality. Always he would step out of his way to kick a stone off the pavement lest somebody should trip over it. If he saw boys quarrelling he stopped to expostulate; and he never could pass a man who was ill-treating a horse without trying to make him behave better. He would never take off his hat to any one, no matter of what rank, nor could he be induced to address any one as "Esquire " or as "Reverend." He would never put on any sign of mourning, even for father and mother; and he adhered to one style of coat and hat throughout all changes of fashion. Improvement was his watchword always and everywhere. Whatever he wrote had to be endlessly corrected, and his love of detail led all his life to his neglecting large ends in his care for small ones. A good heart, but a pedantic conscience, and a sort of energetically mechanical intelligence.

Of himself Herbert Spencer says: "No one will deny that I am much given to criticism. Along with exposition of my own views there has always gone a pointing out of defects in those of others. And if this is a trait in my writing, still more is it a trait in my conversation. The tendency to fault-finding is dominant — disagreeably dominant. The indicating of errors in thought and speech made by those around has all through life been an incurable habit — a habit for which I have often reproached myself, but to no purpose."

The "Autobiography" abounds in illustrations of the habit. For instance : —

"Of late I have observed sundry cases in which, having found the right, people deliberately desert it for the wrong. . . . A generation ago salt-cellars were made of convenient shapes — either ellipses or elongated parallelograms: the advantage being that the salt-spoon, placed lengthwise, remained in its place. But for some time past, fashion has dictated circular salt-cellars, on the edges of which the salt-spoon will not remain without skilful balancing: it falls on the cloth. In my boyhood a jug was made of a form at once convenient and graceful. . . . Now, however, the almost universal form of jug in use is a frustum of a cone with a miniature spout. It combines all possible defects. When anything like full, it is impossible to pour out a small quantity without part of the liquid trickling down beneath the spout; and a larger quantity cannot be poured out without exceeding the limits of the spout and running over on each side of it. If the jug is half empty, the tilting must be continued a long time before any liquid comes; and then, when it does come, it comes with a rush; because its surface has now become so large that a small inclination delivers a great deal. To all which add that the shape is as ugly a one as can well be hit upon. Still more extraordinary is the folly of a change made in another utensil of daily use " — and Spencer goes on to find fault with the cylindrical form of candle extinguisher, proving by a description of its shape that "it squashes the wick into the melted composition, the result being that when, next day, the extinguisher is taken off, the wick, imbedded in the solidified composition, cannot be lighted without difficulty" (vol. ii, page 238).

The remorseless explicitness, the punctuation, everything, make these specimens of public fault-finding with what probably was the equipment of Mr. Spencer's latest boarding-house, sound like passages from "The Man versus the State." Another example: —

"Playing billiards became 'my custom always of the afternoon.' Those who confess to billiard-playing commonly make some kind of an excuse. . . . It suffices to me that I like billiards, and the attainment of the pleasure given I regard as a sufficient motive. I have for a long time deliberately set my face against that asceticism which makes it an offence to do a thing for the pleasure of doing it; and have habitually contended that, so long as no injury is inflicted on others, nor any ulterior injury on self, and so long as the various duties of life have been discharged, the pursuit of pleasure for its own sake is perfectly legitimate and requires no apology. The opposite view is nothing else than a remote sequence of the old devil worship of the barbarian, who sought to please his god by inflicting pains upon himself, and believed his god would he angry if he made himself happy " (vol. ii, page 263).

The tone of pedantic rectitude in these passages is characteristic. Every smallest thing is either right or wrong, and if wrong, can be articulately proved so by reasoning. Life grows too dry and literal, and loses all aërial perspective at such a rate; and the effect is the more displeasing when the matters in dispute have a rich variety of aspects, and when the aspect from which Mr. Spencer deduces his conclusions is manifestly partial.

For instance, in his art-criticisms. Spencer in his youth did much drawing, both mechanical and artistic. Volume one contains a photo-print of a very creditable bust which he modelled of his uncle. He had a musical ear, and practiced singing. He paid attention to style, and was not wholly insensible to poetry. Yet in all his dealings with the art-products of mankind he manifests the same curious dryness and mechanical literality of judgment, — a dryness increased by pride in his nonconformity. He would, for example, rather give a large sum than read to the end of Homer's Iliad, — the ceaseless repetition of battles, speeches, and epithets like well-greaved Greeks, horse-breaking Trojans; the tedious enumeration of details of dresses, arms, and chariots; such absurdities as giving the genealogy of a horse while in the midst of a battle; and the appeals to savage and brutal passions, having soon made the poem intolerable to him (vol. i, page 300). Turner's paintings he finds untrue, in that the earth-region is habitually as bright in tone as the air-region. Moreover, Turner scatters his detail too evenly. In Greek statues the hair is falsely treated. Renaissance painting, even the best, is spoiled by unreal illumination, and non-rendering of reflected light in the shadows. Venetian gothic sins by meaningless ornamentation.

St. Mark's Church may be precious archæo-
logically, but is not æsthetically precious. Of
Wagner's music he admires nothing but the
skilful specialization of the instruments in the
orchestra.

The fault-finding in all these cases rests
on observation, true as far as it goes; but
the total absence of genial relations with the
entirety of the phenomenon discussed, the
clutching at some paltry mechanical aspect
of it that lends itself to reasoned proof by a
plus b, and the practical denial of everything
that only appeals to vaguer sentiment, show
a mind so oddly limited to ratiocinative and
explicit processes, and so wedded to the superficial and flagrantly *insufficient*, that one begins to wonder whether in the philosophic and
scientific spheres the same mind can have
wrought out results of extraordinary value.

Both "yes " and "no " are here the answer.
Every one who writes books or articles knows
how he must flounder until he hits upon the
proper opening. Once the right beginning
found, everything follows easily and in due

order. If a man, however narrow, strikes even by accident, into one of these fertile openings, and pertinaciously follows the lead, he is almost sure to meet truth on his path. Some thoughts act almost like mechanical centres of crystallization; facts cluster of themselves about them. Such a thought was that of the gradual growth of all things, by natural processes, out of natural antecedents. Until the middle of the nineteenth century no one had grasped it *wholesale;* and the thinker who did so earliest was bound to make discoveries just in proportion to the exclusiveness of his interest in the principle. He who had the keenest eye for instances and illustrations, and was least divertible by casual side-curiosity, would score the quickest triumph.

To Spencer is certainly due the immense credit of having been the first to see in evolution an absolutely universal principle. If any one else had grasped its universality, it failed at any rate to grasp him as it grasped Spencer. For Spencer it instantly became "the guiding conception running through and connecting

all the concrete sciences " (vol. ii, page 196).
Here at last was "an object at once large and
distinct enough " to overcome his "constitutional idleness." "With an important and
definite end to achieve, I could work " (vol. i,
page 215). He became, in short, the victim of
a vivid obsession, and for the first time in his
life seems to have grown genuinely ambitious.
Every item of his experience, small or great,
every idea in his mental storehouse, had now
to be considered with reference to its bearing
on the new universal principle. On pages
194–199 of volume two he gives an interesting summary of the way in which all his previous and subsequent ideas moved into harmonious coördination and subordination, when
once he had this universal key to insight. Applying it wholesale as he did, innumerable
truths unobserved till then had to fall into
his gamebag. And his peculiar trick, a prig-
gish infirmity in daily intercourse, of treating
every smallest thing by abstract law, was here
a merit. Add his sleuth-hound scent for what
he was after, and his untiring pertinacity, to

his priority in perceiving the one great truth, and you fully justify the popular estimate of him as one of the world's geniuses, in spite of the fact that the "temperament" of genius, so called, seems to have been so lacking in him.

In one sense, then, Spencer's personal narrowness and dryness were not hindering, but helping conditions of his achievement. Grant that a vast picture *quelconque* had to be made before the details could be made perfect, and a greater richness and receptivity of mind would have resulted in hestitation. The quality would have been better in spots, but the extensiveness would have suffered.

Spencer is thus the philosopher of vastness. Misprised by many specialists, who carp at his technical imperfections, he has nevertheless enlarged the imagination, and set free the speculative mind of countless doctors, engineers, and lawyers, of many physicists and chemists, and of thoughtful laymen generally. He is the philosopher whom those who have no other philosopher can appreciate. To be able to say this of any man is great praise, and gives the "yes" answer to my recent question.

Can the "no" answer be as unhesitatingly uttered? I think so, if one makes the qualitative aspect of Spencer's work undo its quantitative aspect. The luke-warm equable temperament, the narrowness of sympathy and passion, the fondness for mechanical forms of thought, the imperfect receptivity and lack of interest in facts as such, dissevered from their possible connection with a theory; nay, the very vividness itself, the keenness of scent and the pertinacity; these all are qualities which may easily make for second-rateness, and for contentment with a cheap and loosely woven achievement. As Mr. Spencer's "First Principles" is the book which more than any other has spread his popular reputation, I had perhaps better explain what I mean by criticising some of its peculiarities.

I read this book as a youth when it was still appearing in numbers, and was carried away with enthusiasm by the intellectual perspectives which it seemed to open. When a maturer companion, Mr. Charles S. Peirce, attacked it in my presence, I felt spiritually wounded, as by the defacement of a sacred image or picture, though I could not verbally defend it against his criticisms.

Later I have used it often as a text-book with students, and the total outcome of my dealings with it is an exceedingly unfavorable verdict. Apart from the great truth which it enforces, that everything has evolved somehow, and apart from the inevitable stimulating effect of any such universal picture, I regard its teachings as almost a museum of blundering reasoning. Let me try to indicate briefly my grounds for such an opinion.

I pass by the section on the Unknowable, because this part of Mr. Spencer's philosophy has won fewer friends than any other. It consists chiefly of a rehash of Mansel's rehash of Hamilton's "Philosophy of the Conditioned," and has hardly raised its head since John Mill so effectively demolished it. If criticism of our human intellectual constitution is needed, it can be got out of Bradley to-day better than out of

Spencer. The latter's way of reconciling science and religion is, moreover, too absurdly *naïf*. Find, he says, a fundamental abstract truth on which they can agree, and that will reconcile them. Such a truth, he thinks, is that *there is a mystery*. The trouble is that it is over just such common truths that quarrels begin. Did the fact that both believed in the existence of the Pope reconcile Luther and Ignatius Loyola? Did it reconcile the South and the North that both agreed that there were slaves? Religion claims that the "mystery" is interpretable by human reason; "Science," speaking through Spencer, insists that it is not. The admission of the mystery is the very signal for the quarrel. Moreover, for nine hundred and ninety-nine men out of a thousand the sense of mystery is the sense of *more-to-be-known*, not the sense of a More, *not* to be known.

But pass the Unknowable by, and turn to Spencer's famous law of Evolution.

"Science" works with several types of "law." The most frequent and useful type is that of the "elementary law," — that of the composition of forces, that of gravitation, of refraction, and the like. Such laws declare no concrete facts to exist, and make no prophecy as to any actual future. They limit themselves to saying that *if* a certain character be found in any fact, another character will coexist with it or follow it. The usefulness of these laws is proportionate to the extent to which the characters they treat of pervade the world, and to the accuracy with which they are definable.

Statistical laws form another type, and positively declare something about the world of actuality. Although they tell us nothing of the elements of things, either abstract or concrete, they affirm that the resultant of their actions drifts preponderantly in a particular direction. Population tends toward cities; the working classes tend to grow discontented; the available energy of the universe is running down — such laws prophesy the real future *en gros*, but they never help us to predict any particular detail of it.

Spencer's law of Evolution is of the statistical variety. It defines what evolution means, and what dissolution means, and asserts that, although both processes are always going on together, there is in the present phase of the world a drift in favor of evolution. In the first edition of " First Principles " an evolutive change in anything was described as the passage of it from a state of indefinite incoherent homogeneity to a definite coherent heterogeneity. The existence of a drift in this direction in everything Mr. Spencer proves, both by a survey of facts, and by deducing it from certain laws of the elementary type, which he severally names "the instability of the homogeneous," "the multiplication of effects," "segregation," and "equilibration." The two former insure the heterogeneity, while "segregation" brings about the definiteness and coherence, and "equilibration" arrests the process, and determines when dissolutive changes shall begin.

The whole panorama is resplendent for variety and inclusiveness, and has aroused an admiration for philosophy in minds that never admired philosophy before. Like Descartes in earlier days, Spencer aims at a purely mechanical explanation of Nature. The knowable universe is nothing but matter and motion, and its history is nothing but the "redistribution" of these entities. The value of such an explanation for scientific purposes depends altogether on how consistent and exact it is. Every "thing" must be interpreted as a "configuration," every "event" as a change of configuration, every predicate ascribed must be of a geometrical sort. Measured by these requirements of mechanics Spencer's attempt has lamentably failed. His terms are vagueness and ambiguity incarnate, and he seems incapable of keeping the mechanical point of view in mind for five pages consecutively.

"Definite," for example, is hardly a physical idea at all. Every motion and every arrangement of matter is definitely what it is, — a fog or an irregular scrawl, as much so as a billiard ball or a straight line. Spencer means by definiteness in a thing any character that makes it arrest our attention, and forces us to distinguish it from other things. The word with him has a human, not a physical connotation. Definite things, in his book, finally appear merely as *things that men have made separate names for*, so that there is hardly a pretence of the mechanical view being kept. Of course names increase as human history proceeds, so "definiteness" in things must necessarily more and more evolve.

"Coherent," again. This has the definite mechanical meaning of resisting separation, of sticking together; but Spencer plays fast and loose with this meaning. Coherence with him sometimes means *permanence in time*, sometimes such *mutual dependence of parts* as is realized in a widely scattered system of no fixed material configuration; a commercial house, for example, with its "travellers" and ships and cars.

An honestly mechanical reader soon rubs his eyes with bewilderment at the orgy of ambiguity to which he is introduced. Every term in Spencer's fireworks shimmers through a whole spectrum of meanings in order to adapt itself to the successive spheres of evolution to which it must apply. "Integration," for instance. A definite coherence is an Integration; and examples given of integration are the contraction of the solar nebula, the formation of the earth's crust, the calcification of cartilage, the shortening of the body of crabs, the loss of his tail by man, the mutual dependence of plants and animals, the growth of powerful states, the tendency of human occupations to go to distinct localities, the dropping of terminal inflexions in English grammar, the formation of general concepts by the mind, the use of machinery instead of simple tools, the development of "composition " in the fine arts, etc., etc. It is obvious that no one form of the motion of matter characterizes all these facts. The human ones simply embody the more and more successful pursuit of certain ends.

In the second edition of his book, Mr. Spencer supplemented his first formula by a unifying addition, meant to be strictly mechanical.

"Evolution," he now said, "is the progressive integration of matter and dissipation of motion," during which both the matter and the motion undergo the previously designated kinds of change. But this makes the formula worse instead of better. The "dissipation of motion " part of it is simple vagueness, — for what particular motion is "dissipated " when a man or state grows more highly evolved? And the integration of matter belongs only to stellar and geologic evolution. Neither heightened specific gravity, nor greater massiveness, which are the only conceivable integrations of matter, is a mark of the more evolved vital, mental, or social things.

It is obvious that the facts of which Spencer here gives so clumsy an account could all have been set down more simply. First there is solar, and then there is geological evolution, processes accurately describable as integrations in the mechanical sense, namely, as decrease in bulk, or growth in hardness. Then Life appears; and after that neither integration of matter nor dissipation of motion plays any part whatever. The result of life, however, is to fill the world more and more with things displaying *organic unity*. By this is meant any arrangement of which one part helps to keep the other parts in existence. Some organic unities are material, — a sea-urchin, for example, a department store, a civil service, or an ecclesiastical organization. Some are mental, as a "science," a code of laws, or an educational programme. But whether they be material or mental products, organic unities must *accumulate;* for every old one tends to conserve itself, and if successful new ones arise they also "come to stay." The human use of Spencer's adjectives "integrated," "definite," "coherent," here no longer shocks one. We are frankly on teleological ground, and metaphor and vagueness are permissible.

This tendency of organic unities to accumulate when once they are formed is absolutely all the truth I can distill from Spencer's unwieldy account of evolution. It makes a much less gaudy and chromatic picture, but what there is of it is exact.

Countless other criticisms swarm toward my pen, but I have no heart to express them, — it is too sorry an occupation. A word about Spencer's conception of "Force," however, insists on being added; for although it is one of his most essential, it is one of his vaguest ideas.

Over all his special laws of evolution there reigns an absolutely general law, that of the "persistence of force." By this Spencer sometimes means the phenomenal law of conservation of energy, sometimes the metaphysical principle that the quantity of existence is unalterable, sometimes the logical principle that nothing can happen without a reason, sometimes the practical postulate that in the absence of any assignable difference you must call a thing the same. This law is one vast vagueness, of which I can give no clear account; but of his special vaguenesses "mental force" and "social force" are good examples. These manifestations of the universal force, he says, are due to vital force, and this latter is due to physical force, both being proportionate to the amount of physical force which is "transformed" into them. But what on earth is "social force"? Sometimes he identifies it with "social activity" (showing the latter to be proportionate to the amount of food eaten), sometimes with the work done by human beings and their steam-engines, and shows it to be due ultimately to the sun's heat. It would never occur to a reader of his pages that a social force proper might be anything that acted as a stimulus of social change, — a leader, for example, a discovery, a book, a new idea, or a national insult; and that the greatest of "forces" of this kind need embody no more "physical force" than the smallest. The measure of greatness here is the effect produced on the environment, not a quantity antecedently absorbed from physical nature. Mr. Spencer himself is a great social force; but he ate no more than an average man, and his body, if cremated, would disengage no more energy. The effects he exerts are of the nature *of releases*, — his words pull triggers in certain kinds of brain.

The fundamental distinction in mechanics between forces of push-and-pull and forces of release is one of which Mr. Spencer, in his earlier years, made no use whatever. Only in his sixth edition did he show that it had seriously arrested his attention. In biology, psychology, and sociology the forces concerned are almost exclusively forces of release. Spencer's account of social forces is neither good sociology nor good mechanics. His feeble grasp of the conception of force vitiates, in fact, all his work.

But the task of a carper is repugnant. The "Essays," "Biology," "Psychology," "Sociology," and "Ethics" are all better than "First Principles," and contain numerous and admirable bits of penetrating work of detail. My impression is that, of the systematic treatises, the "Psychology" will rank as the most original. Spencer broke new ground here in insisting that, since mind and its environment have evolved together, they must be studied together. He gave to the study of mind in isolation a definitive quietus, and that certainly is a great thing to have achieved. To be sure he overdid the matter, as usual, and left no room for any mental structure at all, except that which passively resulted from the storage of impressions received from the outer world in the order of their frequency by fathers and transmitted to their sons. The belief that whatever is acquired by sires is inherited by sons, and the ignoring of purely inner variations, are weak points; but to have brought in the environment as vital was a master stroke.

I may say that Spencer's controversy over use-inheritance with Weismann, entered into after he was sixty, seems to me in point of quality better than any other part of his work. It is genuine labor over a puzzle, genuine research.

Spencer's "Ethics" is a most vital and original piece of attitude-taking in the world of ideals. His politico-ethical activity in general breathes the purest English spirit of liberty, and his attacks on over-administration and criticisms on the inferiority of great centralized systems are worthy to be the text-books of individualists the world over. I confess that it is with this part of his work, in spite of its hardness and inflexibility of tone, that I personally sympathize most.

Looking back on Mr. Spencer as a whole, as this admirably truth-telling "Autobiography" reveals him, he is a figure unique for quaint consistency. He never varied from that inimitable blend of small and vast mindedness, of liberality and crabbedness, which was his personal note, and which defies our formulating power. If an abstract logical concept could come to life, its life would be like Spencer's, — the same definiteness of exclusion and inclusion, the same bloodlessness of temperament, the same narrowness of intent and vastness of extent, the same power of applying itself to numberless instances. But he was no abstract idea; he was a man vigorously devoted to truth and justice as he saw them, who had deep insights, and who finished, under terrible frus-

141

trations from bad health, a piece of work that, taken for all in all, is extraordinary. A human life is greater than all its possible appraisers, assessors, and critics. In comparison with the fact of Spencer's actual living, such critical characterization of it as I have been at all these pains to produce seems a rather unimportant as well as a decidedly graceless thing.

VII

FREDERIC MYERS'
SERVICES TO PSYCHOLOGY

VII

FREDERIC MYERS'
SERVICES TO PSYCHOLOGY[1]

On this memorial occasion it is from English hearts and tongues belonging, as I never had the privilege of belonging, to the immediate environment of our lamented President, that discourse of him as a man and as a friend must come. It is for those who participated in the endless drudgery of his labors for our Society to tell of the high powers he showed there; and it is for those who have something of his burning interest in the problem of our human destiny to estimate his success in throwing a little more light into its dark recesses. To me it has been deemed best to assign a colder task. Frederic Myers was a psychologist who worked upon lines hardly

[1] Written for a meeting of the Society for Psychical Research held after the death of Frederic Myers and first published in the Society's *Proceedings*, Part XLII, page 17 (1901).

admitted by the more academic branch of the profession to be legitimate; and as for some years I bore the title of "Professor of Psychology," the suggestion has been made (and by me gladly welcomed) that I should spend my portion of this hour in defining the exact place and rank which we must accord to him as a cultivator and promoter of the science of the Mind.

Brought up entirely upon literature and history, and interested at first in poetry and religion chiefly; never by nature a philosopher in the technical sense of a man forced to pursue consistency among concepts for the mere love of the logical occupation; not crammed with science at college, or trained to scientific method by any passage through a laboratory, Myers had as it were to re-create his personality before he became the wary critic of evidence, the skilful handler of hypothesis, the learned neurologist and omnivorous reader of biological and cosmological matter, with whom in later years we were acquainted. The transformation came

146

about because he needed to be all these things in order to work successfully at the problem that lay near his heart; and the ardor of his will and the richness of his intellect are proved by the success with which he underwent so unusual a transformation.

The problem, as you know, was that of seeking evidence for human immortality. His contributions to psychology were incidental to that research, and would probably never have been made had he not entered on it. But they have a value for Science entirely independent of the light they shed upon that problem; and it is quite apart from it that I shall venture to consider them.

If we look at the history of mental science we are immediately struck by diverse tendencies among its several cultivators, the consequence being a certain opposition of schools and some repugnance among their disciples. Apart from the great contrasts between minds that are teleological or biological and minds that are mechanical, between the animists and the associationists in psychology, there is the entirely different contrast between what I will call the classic-academic and the romantic type of imagination. The former has a fondness for clean pure lines and noble simplicity in its constructions. It explains things by as few principles as possible and is intolerant of either nondescript facts or clumsy formulas. The facts must lie in a neat assemblage, and the psychologist must be enabled to cover them and "tuck them in" as safely under his system as a mother tucks her babe in under the down coverlet on a winter night. Until quite recently all psychology, whether animistic or associationistic, was written on classic-academic lines. The consequence was that the human mind, as it is figured in this literature, was largely an abstraction. Its normal adult traits were recognized. A sort of sunlit terrace was exhibited on which it took its exercise. But where that terrace stopped, the mind stopped; and there was nothing farther left to tell of in this kind of philosophy but the brain and the other physical facts of nature on the one hand, and the absolute metaphysical ground of the universe on the other.

But of late years the terrace has been overrun by romantic improvers, and to pass to their work is like going from classic to gothic architecture, where few outlines are pure and where uncouth forms lurk in the shadows. A mass of mental phenomena are now seen in the shrubbery beyond the parapet. Fantastic, ignoble, hardly human, or frankly non-human are some of these new candidates for psychological description. The menagerie and the madhouse, the nursery, the prison, and the hospital, have been made to deliver up their material. The world of mind is shown as something infinitely more complex than was suspected; and whatever beauties it may still possess, it has lost at any rate the beauty of academic neatness.

But despite the triumph of romanticism, psychologists as a rule have still some lingering prejudice in favor of the nobler simplicities. Moreover, there are social prejudices which scientific men themselves obey. The word "hypnotism" has been trailed about in the newspapers so that even we ourselves rather wince at it, and avoid occasions of its use. "Mesmerism," "clairvoyance," "medium," — *horrescimus referentes!* — and with all these things, infected by their previous mystery-mongering discoverers, even our best friends had rather avoid complicity. For instance, I invite eight of my scientific colleagues severally to come to my house at their own time, and sit with a medium for whom the evidence already published in our "Proceedings" had been most noteworthy. Although it means at worst the waste of the hour for each, five of them decline the adventure. I then beg the "Commission" connected with the chair of a certain learned psychologist in a neighboring university to examine the same medium, whom Mr. Hodgson and I offer at our own expense to send and leave with them. They also have to be excused from any such entanglement. I advise another psychological friend to look into this medium's case, but he replies that it is useless; for if he should get such results as I report, he would (being suggestible) simply believe himself hallucinated. When I propose as a remedy that he should remain in the background and take notes, whilst his wife has the sitting, he explains that he can never consent to his wife's presence at such performances. This friend of mine writes *ex cathedra* on the subject of psychical research, declaring (I need hardly add) that there is nothing in it; the chair of the psychologist with the Commission was founded by a spiritist, partly with a view to investigate mediums; and one of the five colleagues who declined my invitation is widely quoted as an effective critic of our evidence. So runs the world away! I should not indulge in the personality and triviality of such anecdotes, were it not that they paint the temper of our time, a temper which, thanks to Frederic Myers more than to any one, will certainly be impossible after this generation. Myers was, I think, decidedly exclusive and intolerant by nature. But his keenness for truth carried him into regions where either intellectual or social squeamishness would have been fatal, so he "mortified" his *amour propre*, unclubbed himself completely, and became a model of patience, tact and humility wherever investigation required it. Both his example and his body of doctrine will make this temper the only one henceforward scientifically respectable.

If you ask me how his doctrine has this effect, I answer: By co-ordinating! For Myers' great principle of research was that in order to understand any one species of fact we ought to have all the species of the same general class of fact before us. So he took a lot of scattered phenomena, some of them recognized as reputable, others outlawed from science, or treated as isolated curiosities; he made series of them, filled in the transitions by delicate hypotheses or analogies; and bound them together in a system by his bold inclusive conception of the Subliminal Self, so that no one can now touch one part of the fabric without finding the rest entangled with it. Such vague terms of apperception as psychologists have hitherto been satisfied with using for most of these phenomena, as "fraud," "rot," "rubbish," will no more be possible hereafter than "dirt" is possible as a head of classification in chemistry, or "vermin" in zoology. Whatever they are, they are things with a right to definite description and to careful observation.

I cannot but account this as a great service rendered to Psychology. I expect that Myers will ere long distinctly figure in mental science as the radical leader in what I have called the romantic movement. Through him for the first time, psychologists are in possession of their full material, and mental phenomena are set down in an adequate inventory. To bring unlike things thus together by forming series of which the intermediary terms connect the extremes, is a procedure much in use by scientific men. It is a first step made towards securing their interest in the romantic facts, that Myers should have shown how easily this familiar method can be applied to their study.

Myers' conception of the extensiveness of the Subliminal Self quite overturns the classic notion of what the human mind consists in. The supraliminal region, as Myers calls it, the classic-academic consciousness, which was once alone considered either by associationists or animists, figures in his theory as only a small segment of the psychic spectrum. It is a special phase of mentality, teleologically evolved for adaptation to our natural environment, and forms only what he calls a "privileged case" of personality. The outlying Subliminal, according to him, represents more fully our central and abiding being.

I think the words subliminal and supraliminal unfortunate, but they were probably unavoidable. I think, too, that Myers' belief in the ubiquity and great extent of the Subliminal will demand a far larger number of facts than sufficed to persuade him, before the next generation of psychologists shall become persuaded. He regards the

Subliminal as the enveloping mother-consciousness in each of us, from which the consciousness we wot of is precipitated like a crystal. But whether this view get confirmed or get overthrown by future inquiry, the definite way in which Myers has thrown it down is a new and specific challenge to inquiry. For half a century now, psychologists have fully admitted the existence of a subliminal mental region, under the name either of unconscious cerebration or of the involuntary life; but they have never definitely taken up the question of the extent of this region, never sought explicitly to map it out. Myers definitely attacks this problem, which, after him, it will be impossible to ignore.

What is the precise constitution of the Subliminal — such is the problem which deserves to figure in our Science hereafter as the *problem of Myers;* and willy-nilly, inquiry must follow on the path which it has opened up. But Myers has not only propounded the problem definitely, he has also invented definite methods for its solution. Posthypnotic suggestion, crystal-gazing, automatic writing and trance-speech, the willing-game, etc., are now, thanks to him, instruments of research, reagents like litmus paper or the galvanometer, for revealing what would otherwise he hidden. These are so many ways of putting the Subliminal on tap. Of course without the simultaneous work on hypnotism and hysteria independently begun by others, he could not have pushed his own work so far. But he is so far the only generalizer of the problem and the only user of all the methods; and even though his theory of the extent of the Subliminal should have to be subverted in the end, its formulation will, I am sure, figure always as a rather momentous event in the history of our Science.

Any psychologist who should wish to read Myers out of the profession — and there are probably still some who would be glad to do so to-day — is committed to a definite alternative. Either he must say that we knew all about the subliminal region before Myers took it up, or he must say that it is certain

that states of super-normal cognition form
no part of its content. The first contention
would be too absurd. The second one remains
more plausible. There are many first hand
investigators into the Subliminal who, not
having themselves met with anything supernormal, would probably not hesitate to call
all the reports of it erroneous, and who would
limit the Subliminal to dissolutive phenomena
of consciousness exclusively, to lapsed memories, subconscious sensations, impulses and
phobias, and the like. Messrs. Janet and
Binet, for aught I know, may hold some such
position as this. Against it Myers' thesis
would stand sharply out. Of the Subliminal,
he would say, we can give no ultra-simple account: there are discreet regions in it, levels
separated by critical points of transition,
and no one formula holds true of them all.
And any conscientious psychologist ought,
it seems to me, to see that, since these
multiple modifications of personality are only
beginning to be reported and observed with
care, it is obvious that a dogmatically nega-

tive treatment of them must be premature, and that the problem of Myers still awaits us as the problem of far the deepest moment for our actual psychology, whether his own tentative solutions of certain parts of it be correct or not.

Meanwhile, descending to detail, one cannot help admiring the great originality with which Myers wove such an extraordinarily detached and discontinuous series of phenomena together. Unconscious cerebration, dreams, hypnotism, hysteria, inspirations of genius, the willing-game, planchette, crystal-gazing, hallucinatory voices, apparitions of the dying, medium-trances, demoniacal possession, clairvoyance, thought-transference, even ghosts and other facts more doubtful; these things form a chaos at first sight most discouraging. No wonder that scientists can think of no other principle of unity among them than their common appeal to men's perverse propensity to superstition. Yet Myers has actually made a system of them, stringing them continuously upon a perfectly legitimate objective hypothesis, verified in some cases and extended to others by analogy. Taking the name "automatism" from the phenomenon of automatic writing — I am not sure that he may not himself have been the first so to baptize this latter phenomenon — he made one great simplification at a stroke by treating hallucinations and active impulses under a common head, as *sensory* and *motor automatisms*. Automatism he then conceived broadly as a message of any kind from the Subliminal to the Supraliminal. And he went a step farther in his hypothetic interpretation, when he insisted on "symbolism" as one of the ways in which one stratum of our personality will often interpret the influences of another. Obsessive thoughts and delusions, as well as voices, visions, and impulses, thus fall subject to one mode of treatment. To explain them, we must explore the Subliminal; to cure them we must practically influence it.

Myers' work on automatism led to his brilliant conception, in 1891, of hysteria. He defined it, with good reasons given, as "a disease of the hypnotic stratum." Hardly had he done so when the wonderfully ingenious observations of Binet, and especially of Janet in France, gave to this view the completest of corroborations. These observations have been extended in Germany, America, and elsewhere; and although Binet and Janet worked independently of Myers, and did work far more objective, he nevertheless will stand as the original announcer of a theory which, in my opinion, makes an epoch, not only in medical but in psychological science, because it brings in an entirely new conception of our mental possibilities.

Myers' manner of apprehending the problem of the Subliminal shows itself fruitful in every possible direction. While official science practically refuses to attend to Subliminal phenomena, the circles which do attend to them treat them with a respect altogether too undiscriminating, — every Subliminal deliverance must be an oracle. The result is that there is no basis of intercourse between those who best know the facts and those who are most competent to discuss them. Myers immediately establishes a basis by his remark that in so far as they have to use the same organism, with its preformed avenues of expression — what may be very different strata of the Subliminal are condemned in advance to manifest themselves in similar ways. This might account for the great generic likeness of so many automatic performances, while their different starting-points behind the threshold might account for certain differences in them. Some of them, namely, seem to include elements of supernormal knowledge; others to show a curious subconscious mania for personation and deception; others again to be mere drivel. But Myers' conception of various strata or levels in the Subliminal sets us to analyzing them all from a new point of view. The word Subliminal for him denotes only a region, with possibly the most heterogeneous contents. Much of the content is certainly rubbish, matter that Myers calls dissolutive, stuff that dreams are made of, fragments of lapsed memory, mechanical effects of habit and ordinary suggestion; some belongs to a middle region where a strange manufacture of inner romances perpetually goes on; finally, some of the content appears superiorly and subtly perceptive. But each has to appeal to us by the same channels and to use organs partly trained to their performance by messages from the other levels. Under these conditions what could be more natural to expect than a confusion which Myers' suggestion would then have been the first indispensable step towards finally clearing away.

Once more, then, whatever be the upshot of the patient work required here, Myers' resourceful intellect has certainly done a service to psychology.

I said a while ago that his intellect was not by nature philosophic in the narrower sense of being that of a logician. In the broader sense of being a man of wide scientific imagination, Myers was most eminently a philosopher. He has shown this by his unusually daring grasp of the principle of evolution, and by the wonderful way in which he has worked out suggestions of mental evolution by means of biological analogies. These analogies are, if anything, too profuse and dazzling in his pages; but his conception of mental evolution is more radical than anything yet considered by psychologists as possible. It is absolutely original; and, being so radical, it becomes one of those hypotheses which, once propounded, can never be forgotten, but sooner or later have to be worked out and submitted in every way to criticism and verification.

The corner-stone of his conception is the fact that consciousness has no essential unity. It aggregates and dissipates, and what we call normal consciousness, — the "Human Mind" of classic psychology, — is not even typical, but only one case out of thousands. Slight organic alterations, intoxications, and auto-intoxications, give supraliminal forms completely different, and the subliminal region seems to have laws in many respects peculiar. Myers thereupon makes the suggestion that the whole system of consciousness studied by the classic psychology is only an extract from a larger total, being a part told-off, as it were, to do service in the adjustments of our physical organism to the world of nature. This extract, aggregated and personified for this particular purpose, has, like all evolving things, a variety of peculiarities. Having evolved, it may also dissolve, and in dreams, hysteria, and divers forms of degeneration it seems to do so. This is a retrograde process of separation in a consciousness of which the unity was once effected. But again the consciousness may follow the opposite course and integrate still farther, or evolve by growing into yet untried directions. In veridical automatisms it actually seems to do so. It drops some of its usual modes of increase, its ordinary use of the senses, for example, and lays hold of bits of information which, in ways that we cannot even follow conjecturally, leak into it by way of the Subliminal. The ulterior source of a certain part of this information (limited and perverted as it

always is by the organism's idiosyncrasies
in the way of transmission and expression)
Myers thought he could reasonably trace
to departed human intelligence, or its existing equivalent. I pretend to no opinion on
this point, for I have as yet studied the evidence with so little critical care that Myers
was always surprised at my negligence. I
can therefore speak with detachment from
this question and, as a mere empirical psychologist, of Myers' general evolutionary
conception. As such a psychologist I feel
sure that the latter is a hypothesis of first-
rate philosophic importance. It is based, of
course, on his convicton of the extent of the
Subliminal, and will stand or fall as that is
verified or not; but whether it stand or fall,
it looks to me like one of those sweeping ideas
by which the scientific researches of an entire
generation are often moulded. It would not
be surprising if it proved such a leading idea
in the investigation of the near future; for
in one shape or another, the Subliminal has
come to stay with us, and the only possible

course to take henceforth is radically and thoroughly to explore its significance.

Looking back from Frederic Myers' vision of vastness in the field of psychological research upon the programme as most academic psychologists frame it, one must confess that its limitation at their hands seems not only unplausible, but in truth, a little ridiculous. Even with brutes and madmen, even with hysterics and hypnotics admitted as the academic psychologists admit them, the official outlines of the subject are far too neat to stand in the light of analogy with the rest of Nature. The ultimates of Nature, — her simple elements, if there be such, — may indeed combine in definite proportions and follow classic laws of architecture; but in her proximates, in her phenomena as we immediately experience them, Nature is everywhere gothic, not classic. She forms a real jungle, where all things are provisional, half-fitted to each other, and untidy. When we add such a complex kind of subliminal region as Myers believed in to the official region, we restore the analogy; and, though we may be mistaken in much detail, in a general way, at least, we become plausible. In comparison with Myers' way of attacking the question of immortality in particular, the official way is certainly so far from the mark as to be almost preposterous. It assumes that when our ordinary consciousness goes out, the only alternative surviving kind of consciousness that could be possible is abstract mentality, living on spiritual truth, and communicating ideal wisdom — in short, the whole classic platonizing Sunday-school conception. Failing to get that sort of thing when it listens to reports about mediums, it denies that there can be anything. Myers approaches the subject with no such *a priori* requirement. If he finds any positive indication of "spirits," he records it, whatever it may be, and is willing to fit his conception to the facts, however grotesque the latter may appear, rather than to blot out the facts to suit his conception. But, as was long ago said by our collaborator, Mr. Canning Schiller, in words more effective than any I can write, if any conception should be blotted out by serious lovers of Nature, it surely ought to be classic academic Sunday-school conception. If anything is unlikely in a world like this, it is that the next adjacent thing to the mere surface-show of our experience should be the realm of eternal essences, of platonic ideas, of crystal battlements, of absolute significance. But whether they be animists or associationists, a supposition something like this is still the assumption of our usual psychologists. It comes from their being for the most part philosophers, in the technical sense, and from their showing the weakness of that profession for logical abstractions. Myers was primarily a lover of life and not of abstractions. He loved human life, human persons, and their peculiarities. So he could easily admit the possibility of level beyond level of perfectly concrete experience, all "queer and cactus-like" though it might be, before we touch the absolute, or reach the eternal essences.

Behind the minute anatomists and the physiologists, with their metallic instruments, there have always stood the out-door naturalists with their eyes and love of concrete nature. The former call the latter superficial, but there is something wrong about your laboratory-biologist who has no sympathy with living animals. In psychology there is a similar distinction. Some psychologists are fascinated by the varieties of mind in living action, others by the dissecting out, whether by logical analysis or by brass instruments, of whatever elementary mental processes may be there. Myers must decidedly be placed in the former class, though his powerful use of analogy enabled him also to do work after the fashion of the latter. He loved human nature as Cuvier and Agassiz loved animal nature; in his view, as in their view, the subject formed a vast living picture. Whether his name will have in psychology as honorable a place as their names have gained in the sister science, will depend on whether future inquirers shall adopt or reject his theories;

and the rapidity with which their decision shapes itself will depend largely on the vigor with which this Society continues its labor in his absence. It is at any rate a possibility, and I am disposed to think it a probability, that Frederic Myers will always be remembered in psychology as the pioneer who staked out a vast tract of mental wilderness and planted the flag of genuine science upon it. He was an enormous collector. He introduced for the first time comparison, classification, and serial order into the peculiar kind of fact which he collected. He was a genius at perceiving analogies; he was fertile in hypotheses; and as far as conditions allowed it in this meteoric region, he relied on verification. Such advantages are of no avail, however, if one has struck into a false road from the outset. But should it turn out that Frederic Myers has really hit the right road by his divining instinct, it is certain that, like the names of others who have been wise, his name will keep an honorable place in scientific history.

VIII

FINAL IMPRESSIONS OF A
PSYCHICAL RESEARCHER

VIII

FINAL IMPRESSIONS OF A PSYCHICAL RESEARCHER[1]

THE late Professor Henry Sidgwick was celebrated for the rare mixture of ardor and critical judgment which his character exhibited. The liberal heart which he possessed had to work with an intellect which acted destructively on almost every particular object of belief that was offered to its acceptance. A quarter of a century ago, scandalized by the chaotic state of opinion regarding the phenomena now called by the rather ridiculous name of "psychic" — phenomena, of which the supply reported seems inexhaustible, but which scientifically trained minds mostly re-

---

[1] Published under the title "Confidences of a Psychical Researcher" in the *American Magazine*, October, 1909. For a more complete and less popular statement of some theories suggested in this article see the last pages of a "Report on Mrs. Piper's Hodgson-Control" in *Proceedings of the [Eng.] Society for Psychical Research*, 1909, 470; also printed in *Proc. of Am. Soc. for Psychical Research* for the same year.

fuse to look at — he established, along with
Professor Barrett, Frederic Myers and Ed-
mund Gurney, the Society for Psychical Research. These men hoped that if the material
were treated rigorously, and, as far as possible,
experimentally, objective truth would be elic-
ited, and the subject rescued from sentimental-
ism on the one side and dogmatizing ignorance
on the other. Like all founders, Sidgwick
hoped for a certain promptitude of result;
and I heard him say, the year before his
death, that if anyone had told him at the outset that after twenty years he would be in the
same identical state of doubt and balance that
he started with, he would have deemed the
prophecy incredible. It appeared impossible
that that amount of handling evidence should
bring so little finality of decision.

My own experience has been similar to
Sidgwick's. For twenty-five years I have
been in touch with the literature of psychical
research, and have had acquaintance with
numerous "researchers." I have also spent a
good many hours (though far fewer than I

ought to have spent) in witnessing (or trying to witness) phenomena. Yet I am theoretically no "further" than I was at the beginning; and I confess that at times I have been tempted to believe that the Creator has eternally intended this department of nature to remain *baffling*, to prompt our curiosities and hopes and suspicions all in equal measure, so that, although ghosts and clairvoyances, and raps and messages from spirits, are always seeming to exist and can never be fully explained away, they also can never be susceptible of full corroboration.

The peculiarity of the case is just that there are so many sources of possible deception in most of the observations that the whole lot of them *may* be worthless, and yet that in comparatively few cases can aught more fatal than this vague general possibility of error be pleaded against the record. Science meanwhile needs something more than bare possibilities to build upon; so your genuinely scientific inquirer — I don't mean your ignoramus "scientist" — has to remain unsatisfied. It is hard to believe, however, that the Creator has really put any big array of phenomena into the world merely to defy and mock our scientific tendencies; so my deeper belief is that we psychical researchers have been too precipitate with our hopes, and that we must expect to mark progress not by quarter-centuries, but by half-centuries or whole centuries.

I am strengthened in this belief by my impression that just at this moment a faint but distinct step forward is being taken by competent opinion in these matters. "Physical phenomena" (movements of matter without contact, lights, hands and faces "materialized," etc.) have been one of the most baffling regions of the general field (or perhaps one of the least baffling *prima facie*, so certain and great has been the part played by fraud in their production); yet even here the balance of testimony seems slowly to be inclining towards admitting the supernaturalist view. Eusapia Paladino, the Neapolitan medium, has been under observation for twenty years or more. Schiaparelli, the astronomer, and Lombroso were the first scientific men to be converted by her performances. Since then innumerable men of scientific standing have seen her, including many "psychic" experts. Every one agrees that she cheats in the most barefaced manner whenever she gets an opportunity. The Cambridge experts, with the Sidgwicks and Richard Hodgson at their head, rejected her *in toto* on that account. Yet her credit has steadily risen, and now her last converts are the eminent psychiatrist, Morselli, the eminent physiologist, Botazzi, and our own psychical researcher, Carrington, whose book on "The Physical Phenomena of Spiritualism" (*against* them rather!) makes his conquest strategically important. If Mr. Podmore, hitherto the prosecuting attorney of the S. P. R., so far as physical phenomena are concerned becomes converted also, we may indeed sit up and look around us. Getting a good health bill from "Science," Eusapia will then throw retrospective credit on Home and Stainton Moses, Florence Cook (Prof. Crookes' medium), and all smilar wonder-workers. The

177

balance of *presumptions* will be changed in favor of genuineness being possible at least, in all reports of this particularly crass and low type of supernatural phenomena.

Not long after Darwin's "Origin of Species" appeared I was studying with that excellent anatomist and man, Jeffries Wyman, at Harvard. He was a convert, yet so far a half-hesitating one, to Darwin's views; but I heard him make a remark that applies well to the subject I now write about. When, he said, a theory gets propounded over and over again, coming up afresh after each time orthodox criticism has buried it, and each time seeming solider and harder to abolish, you may be sure that there is truth in it. Oken and Lamarck and Chambers had been triumphantly despatched and buried, but here was Darwin making the very same heresy seem only more plausible. How often has "Science" killed off all spook philosophy, and laid ghosts and raps and "telepathy" away underground as so much popular delusion. Yet never before

178

were these things offered us so voluminously, and never in such authentic-seeming shape or with such good credentials. The tide seems steadily to be rising, in spite of all the expedients of scientific orthodoxy. It is hard not to suspect that here may be something different from a mere chapter in human gullibility. It may be a genuine realm of natural phenomena.

Falsus in uno, falsus in omnibus, once a cheat, always a cheat, such has been the motto of the English psychical researchers in dealing with mediums. I am disposed to think that, as a matter of policy, it has been wise. Tactically, it is far better to believe much too little than a little too much; and the exceptional credit attaching to the row of volumes of the S. P. R.'s Proceedings, is due to the fixed intention of the editors to proceed very slowly. Better a little belief tied fast, better a small investment *salted down,* than a mass of comparative insecurity.

But, however wise as a policy the S. P. R.'s maxim may have been, as a test of truth, I believe it to be almost irrelevant. In most things human the accusation of deliberate fraud and falsehood is grossly superficial. Man's character is too sophistically mixed for the alternative of "honest or dishonest" to be a sharp one. Scientific men themselves will cheat — at public lectures — rather than let experiments obey their well-known tendency towards failure. I have heard of a lecturer on physics, who had taken over the apparatus of the previous incumbent, consulting him about a certain machine intended to show that, however the peripheral parts of it might be agitated, its centre of gravity remained immovable. "It *will* wobble," he complained. "Well," said the predecessor, apologetically, "to tell the truth, whenever *I* used that machine I found it advisable to *drive a nail* through the centre of gravity." I once saw a distinguished physiologist, now dead, cheat most shamelessly at a public lecture, at the expense of a poor rabbit, and all for the sake of being able to make a cheap joke about its being an "American rabbit" — for no other, he said, could survive such a wound as he pretended to have given it.

To compare small men with great, I have myself cheated shamelessly. In the early days of the Sanders Theater at Harvard, I once had charge of a heart on the physiology of which Professor Newell Martin was giving a popular lecture. This heart, which belonged to a turtle, supported an index-straw which threw a moving shadow, greatly enlarged, upon the screen, while the heart pulsated. When certain nerves were stimulated, the lecturer said, the heart would act in certain ways which he described. But the poor heart was too far gone and, although it stopped duly when the nerve of arrest was excited, that was the final end of its life's tether. Presiding over the performance, I was terrified at the fiasco, and found myself suddenly acting like one of those military geniuses who on the field of battle convert disaster into victory. There was no time for deliberation; so, with my forefinger under a part of the straw that cast no shadow, I found myself impulsively and automatically imitating the rhythmical movements which my colleague had prophesied the

181

heart would undergo. I kept the experiment from failing; and not only saved my colleague (and the turtle) from a humiliation that but for my presence of mind would have been their lot, but I established in the audience the true view of the subject. The lecturer was stating this; and the misconduct of one half-dead specimen of heart ought not to destroy the impression of his words. "There is no worse lie than a truth misunderstood," is a maxim which I have heard ascribed to a former venerated President of Harvard. The heart's failure would have been misunderstood by the audience and given the lie to the lecturer. It was hard enough to make them understand the subject anyhow; so that even now as I write in cool blood I am tempted to think that I acted quite correctly. I was acting for the *larger* truth, at any rate, however automatically; and my sense of this was probably what prevented the more pedantic and literal part of my conscience from checking the action of my sympathetic finger. To this day the memory of that critical emergency has made me feel charitable towards all mediums who make phenomena come in one way when they won't come easily in another. On the principles of the S. P. R., my conduct on that one occasion ought to discredit everything I ever do, everything, for example, I may write in this article, — a manifestly unjust conclusion.

Fraud, conscious or unconscious, seems ubiquitous throughout the range of physical phenomena of spiritism, and false pretence, prevarication and fishing for clues are ubiquitous in the mental manifestations of mediums. If it be not everywhere fraud simulating reality, one is tempted to say, then the reality (if any reality there be) has the bad luck of being fated everywhere to simulate fraud. The suggestion of humbug seldom stops, and mixes itself with the best manifestations. Mrs. Piper's control, "Rector," is a most impressive personage, who discerns in an extraordinary degree his sitter's inner needs, and is capable of giving elevated counsel to fastidious and critical minds. Yet in many respects he is an arrant humbug — such he seems to me at least — pretending to a knowledge and power to which he has no title, nonplussed by contradiction, yielding to suggestion, and covering his tracks with plausible excuses. Now the non-"researching" mind looks upon such phenomena simply according to their face-pretension and never thinks of asking what they may signify below the surface. Since they profess for the most part to be revealers of spirit life, it is either as being absolutely that, or as being absolute frauds, that they are judged. The result is an inconceivably shallow state of public opinion on the subject. One set of persons, emotionally touched at hearing the names of their loved ones given, and consoled by assurances that they are "happy," accept the revelation, and consider spiritualism "beautiful." More hard-headed subjects, disgusted by the revelation's contemptible contents, outraged by the fraud, and prejudiced beforehand against all "spirits," high or low, avert their minds from what they call such "rot" or "bosh" entirely. Thus do two opposite sentimentalisms divide opinion between them! A good expression of the "scientific" state of mind occurs in Huxley's "Life and Letters":

"I regret," he writes, "that I am unable to accept the invitation of the Committee of the Dialectical Society. . . . I take no interest in the subject. The only case of 'Spiritualism' I have ever had the opportunity of examining into for myself was as gross an imposture as ever came under my notice. But supposing these phenomena to be genuine — they do not interest me. If anybody would endow me with the faculty of listening to the chatter of old women and curates in the nearest provincial town, I should decline the privilege, having better things to do. And if the folk in the spiritual world do not talk more wisely and sensibly than their friends report them to do, I put them in the same category. The only good that I can see in the demonstration of the 'Truth of Spiritualism' is to furnish an additional argument against suicide. Better live a crossing-sweeper, than die and be made to talk twaddle by a 'medium' hired at a guinea a *Seance*."[1]

Obviously the mind of the excellent Huxley has here but two whole-souled categories, namely revelation or imposture, to apperceive the case by. Sentimental reasons bar revelation out, for the messages, he thinks, are not romantic enough for that; fraud exists anyhow; therefore the whole thing is nothing but imposture. The odd point is that so few of those who talk in this way realize that they and the spiritists are using the same major premise and differing only in the minor. The major premise is: "Any spirit-revelation must be romantic." The minor of the spiritist is: "This *is* romantic"; that of the Huxleyan is: "this is dingy twaddle" — whence their opposite conclusions!

Meanwhile the first thing that anyone learns who attends seriously to these phenomena is that their causation is far too complex for our feelings about what is or is not romantic enough to be spiritual to throw any light upon

[1] T. H. Huxley, "Life and Letters," I, 240.

it. The causal factors must be carefully distinguished and traced through series, from their simplest to their strongest forms, before we can begin to understand the various resultants in which they issue. Myers and Gurney began this work, the one by his serial study of the various sorts of "automatism," sensory and motor, the other by his experimental proofs that a split-off consciousness may abide after a post-hypnotic suggestion has been given. Here we have subjective factors; but are not transsubjective or objective forces also at work? Veridical messages, apparitions, movements without contact, seem *prima facie* to be such. It was a good stroke on Gurney's part to construct a theory of apparitions which brought the subjective and the objective factors into harmonious co-operation. I doubt whether this telepathic theory of Gurney's will hold along the whole line of apparitions to which he applied it, but it is unquestionable that some theory of that mixed type is required for the explanation of all mediumistic phenomena; and that when all the phsycological factors and elements involved have been told off — and they are many — the question still forces itself upon us: Are these all, or are there indications of any residual forces acting on the subject from beyond, or of any "meta-psychic" faculty (to use Richet's useful term), exerted by him? This is the problem that requires real expertness, and this is where the simple sentimentalisms of the spiritist and scientist leave us in the lurch completely.

"Psychics" form indeed a special branch of education, in which experts are only gradually becoming developed. The phenomena are as massive and wide-spread as is anything in Nature, and the study of them is as tedious, repellent and undignified. To reject it for its unromantic character is like rejecting bacteri-ology because *penicillium glaucum* grows on horse-dung and *bacterium termo* lives in putre-faction. Scientific men have long ago ceased to think of the dignity of the materials they work in. When imposture has been checked off as far as possible, when chance coincidence has been allowed for, when opportunities for normal knowledge on the part of the subject have been noted, and skill in "fishing " and following clues unwittingly furnished by the voice or face of bystanders have been counted in, those who have the fullest acquaintance with the phenomena admit that in good mediums *there is a residuum of knowledge displayed* that can only be called supernormal: the medium taps some source of information not open to ordinary people. Myers used the word "telepathy " to indicate that the sitter's own thoughts or feelings may be thus directly tapped. Mrs. Sidgwick has suggested that if living minds can be thus tapped telepathically, so possibly may the minds of spirits be similarly tapped — if spirits there be. On this view we should have one distinct theory of the performances of a typical test-medium. They would be all originally due to an odd *tendency to personate*, found in her dream life as it expresses itself in trance. [Most of us reveal such a tendency whenever we handle a "ouija-board " or a "planchet," or let ourselves write automatically with a pencil.] The result is a

189

"control," who purports to be speaking; and all the resources of the automatist, including his or her trance-faculty of telepathy, are called into play in building this fictitious personage out plausibly. On such a view of the control, the medium's *will to personate* runs the whole show; and if spirits be involved in it at all, they are passive beings, stray bits of whose memory she is able to seize and use for her purposes, without the spirit being any more aware of it than the sitter is aware of it when his own mind is similarly tapped.

This is one possible way of interpreting a certain type of psychical phenomenon. It uses psychological as well as "spiritual" factors, and quite obviously it throws open for us far more questions than it answers, questions about our subconscious constitution and its curious tendency to humbug, about the telepathic faculty, and about the possibility of an existent spirit-world.

I do not instance this theory to defend it, but simply to show what complicated hypotheses one is inevitably led to consider, the moment one looks at the facts in their complexity and turns one's back on the *naïve* alternative of "revelation or imposture," which is as far as either spiritist thought or ordinary scientist thought goes. The phenomena are endlessly complex in their factors, and they are so little understood as yet that off-hand judgments, whether of "spirits" or of "bosh" are the one as silly as the other. When we complicate the subject still farther by considering what connection such things as rappings, apparitions, poltergeists, spirit-photographs, and materializations may have with it, the bosh end of the scale gets heavily loaded, it is true, but your genuine inquirer still is loath to give up. He lets the data collect, and bides his time. He believes that "bosh" is no more an ultimate element in Nature, or a really explanatory category in human life than "dirt" is in chemistry. Every kind of "bosh" has its own factors and laws; and patient study will bring them definitely to light.

The only way to rescue the "pure bosh" view of the matter is one which has sometimes appealed to my own fancy, but which I imagine few readers will seriously adopt. If, namely, one takes the theory of evolution radically, one ought to apply it not only to the rock-strata, the animals and the plants, but to the stars, to the chemical elements, and to the laws of nature. There must have been a far-off antiquity, one is then tempted to suppose, when things were really chaotic. Little by little, out of all the haphazard possibilities of that time, a few connected things and habits arose, and the rudiments of regular performance began. Every variation in the way of law and order added itself to this nucleus, which inevitably grew more considerable as history went on; while the aberrant and inconstant variations, not being similarly preserved, disappeared from being, wandered off as unrelated vagrants, or else remained so imperfectly connected with the part of the world that had grown regular as only to manifest their existence by occasional lawless intrusions, like those which "psychic" phenomena now make into our scientifically organized world. On such a view, these phenomena ought to remain "pure bosh" forever, that is, they ought to be forever intractable to intellectual methods, because they should not yet be organized enough in themselves to follow any laws. Wisps and shreds of the original chaos, they would be connected enough with the cosmos to affect its periphery every now and then, as by a momentary whiff or touch or gleam, but not enough ever to be followed up and hunted down and bagged. Their relation to the cosmos would be tangential solely.

Looked at dramatically, most occult phenomena make just this sort of impression. They are inwardly as incoherent as they are outwardly wayward and fitful. If they express anything, it is pure "bosh," pure discontinuity, accident, and disturbance, with no law apparent but to interrupt, and no purpose but to baffle. They seem like stray vestiges of that primordial irrationality, from which all our rationalities have been evolved.

To settle dogmatically into this bosh-view would save labor, but it would go against too

many intellectual prepossessions to be adopted
save as a last resort of despair. Your psychical researcher therefore bates no jot of hope,
and has faith that when we get our data numerous enough, some sort of rational treatment
of them will succeed.

When I hear good people say (as they often
say, not without show of reason), that dabbling in such phenomena reduces us to a sort
of jelly, disintegrates the critical faculties,
liquifies the character, and makes of one a
gobe-mouche generally, I console myself by
thinking of my friends Frederic Myers and
Richard Hodgson. These men lived exclusively for psychical research, and it converted
both to spiritism. Hodgson would have been
a man among men anywhere; but I doubt
whether under any other baptism he would
have been that happy, sober and righteous
form of energy which his face proclaimed
him in his later years, when heart and head
alike were wholly satisfied by his occupation.
Myers' character also grew stronger in every
particular for his devotion to the same inquir-

ies.   Brought up on literature and sentiment, something of a courtier, passionate, disdainful, and impatient naturally, he was made over again from the day when he took up psychical research seriously.   He became learned in science, circumspect, democratic in sympathy, endlessly patient, and above all, happy.   The fortitude of his last hours touched the heroic, so completely were the atrocious sufferings of his body cast into insignificance by his interest in the cause he lived for.   When a man's pursuit gradually makes his face shine and grow handsome, you may be sure it is a worthy one.   Both Hodgson and Myers kept growing ever handsomer and stronger-looking.

Such personal examples will convert no one, and of course they ought not to.   Nor do I seek at all in this article to convert any one to my belief that psychical research is an important branch of science.   To do that, I should have to quote evidence; and those for whom the volumes of S. P. R. "Proceedings" already published count for nothing would remain in their dogmatic slumber, though one rose from the dead. No, not to convert readers, but simply to *put my own state of mind upon record publicly* is the purpose of my present writing. Some one said to me a short time ago, that after my twenty-five years of dabbling in "Psychics," it would be rather shameful were I unable to state any definite conclusions whatever as a consequence. I had to agree; so I now proceed to take up the challenge and express such convictions as have been engendered in me by that length of experience, be the same true or false ones. I may be dooming myself to the pit in the eyes of better-judging posterity; I may be raising myself to honor; I am willing to take the risk, for what I shall write is *my* truth, as I now see it.

I began this article by confessing myself baffled. I *am* baffled, as to spirit-return, and as to many other special problems. I am also constantly baffled as to what to think of this or that particular story, for the sources of error in any one observation are seldom fully knowable. But weak sticks make strong faggots; and when the stories fall into consistent sorts that point each in a definite direction, one gets a sense of being in presence of genuinely natural types of phenomena. As to there being such real natural types of phenomena ignored by orthodox science, I am not baffled at all, for I am fully convinced of it. One cannot get demonstrative proof here. One has to follow one's personal sense, which, of course, is liable to err, of the dramatic probabilities of nature. Our critics here obey their sense of dramatic probability as much as we do. Take "raps" for example, and the whole business of objects moving without contact. "Nature," thinks the scientific man, is not so unutterably silly. The cabinet, the darkness, the tying, suggest a sort of human rat-hole life exclusively and "swindling" is for him the dramatically sufficient explanation. It probably is, in an indefinite majority of instances; yet it is to me dramatically improbable that the swindling should not have accreted round some originally genuine nucleus. If we look at human imposture as a historic phenomenon, we find it always imitative. One swindler imitates a previous swindler, but the first swindler of that kind imitated some one who was honest. You can no more create an absolutely new trick than you can create a new word without any previous basis. — You don't know how to go about it. Try, reader, yourself, to invent an unprecedented kind of "physical phenomenon of spiritualism." When *I* try, I find myself mentally turning over the regular medium-stock, and thinking how I might improve some item. This being the dramatically probable human way, I think differently of the whole type, taken collectively, from the way in which I may think of the single instance. I find myself believing that there is "something in" these never ending reports of physical phenomena, although I have n't yet the least positive notion of the something. It becomes to my mind simply a very worthy problem for investigation. Either I or the scientist is of course a fool, with our opposite views of probability here; and I only wish he might feel the liability, as cordially as I do, to pertain to both of us.

I fear I look on Nature generally with more charitable eyes than his, though perhaps he would pause if he realized as I do, how vast the fraudulency is which inconsistency he must attribute to her. Nature is brutal enough, Heaven knows; but no one yet has held her non-human side to be *dishonest*, and even in the human sphere deliberate deceit is far rarer than the "classic" intellect, with its few and rigid categories, was ready to acknowledge. There is a hazy penumbra in us all where lying and delusion meet, where passion rules beliefs as well as conduct, and where the term "scoundrel" does not clear up everything to the depths as it did for our forefathers. The first automatic writing I ever saw was forty years ago. I unhesitatingly thought of it as deceit, although it contained vague elements of supernormal knowledge. Since then I have come to see in automatic writing one example of a department of human activity as vast as it is enigmatic. Every sort of per-

son is liable to it, or to something equivalent
to it; and whoever encourages it in himself
finds himself personating someone else, either
signing what he writes by fictitious name, or
spelling out, by ouija-board or table-tips, messages from the departed. Our subconscious
region seems, as a rule, to be dominated either
by a crazy "will to make-believe," or by some
curious external force impelling us to personation. The first difference between the
psychical researcher and the inexpert person
is that the former realizes the commonness
and typicality of the phenomenon here, while
the latter, less informed, thinks it so rare as to
be unworthy of attention. *I wish to go on
record for the commonness.*

The next thing I wish to go on record for is
the presence, in the midst of all the humbug,
of really supernormal knowledge. By this I
mean knowledge that cannot be traced to the
ordinary sources of information — the senses
namely, of the automatist. In really strong
mediums this knowledge seems to be abundant,
though it is usually spotty, capricious and

unconnected. Really strong mediums are rarities; but when one starts with them and works downwards into less brilliant regions of the automatic life, one tends to interpret many slight but odd coincidences with truth as possibly rudimentary forms of this kind of knowledge.

What is one to think of this queer chapter in human nature? It is odd enough on any view. If all it means is a preposterous and inferior monkey-like tendency to forge messages, systematically embedded in the soul of all of us, it is weird; and weirder still that it should then own all this supernormal information. If on the other hand the supernormal information be the key to the phenomenon, it ought to be superior; and then how ought we to account for the "wicked partner," and for the undeniable mendacity and inferiority of so much of the performance? We are thrown, for our conclusions, upon our instinctive sense of the dramatic probabilities of nature. My own dramatic sense tends instinctively to picture the situation as an interaction between slumbering faculties in the automatist's mind and a cosmic environment of *other conscious-ness* of some sort which is able to work upon them. If there were in the universe a lot of diffuse soul-stuff, unable of itself to get into consistent personal form, or to take permanent possession of an organism, yet always craving to do so, it might get its head into the air, para-sitically, so to speak, by profiting by weak spots in the armor of human minds, and slip-ping in and stirring up there the sleeping ten-dency to personate. It would induce habits in the subconscious region of the mind it used thus, and would seek above all things to pro-long its social opportunities by making itself agreeable and plausible. It would drag stray scraps of truth with it from the wider envi-ronment, but would betray its mental inferi-ority by knowing little how to weave them into any important or significant story.

This, I say, is the dramatic view which my mind spontaneously takes, and it has the ad-vantage of falling into line with ancient human traditions. The views of others are just as dramatic, *for the phenomenon is actuated by will of some sort anyhow*, and wills give rise to dramas. The spiritist view, as held by Messrs. Hyslop and Hodgson, sees a "will to communicate," struggling through inconceivable layers of obstruction in the conditions. I have heard Hodgson liken the difficulties to those of two persons who on earth should have only dead-drunk servants to use as their messengers. The scientist, for his part, sees a "will to deceive," watching its chance in all of us, and able (possibly?) to use "telepathy" in its service.

Which kind of will, and how many kinds of will are most inherently probable? Who can say with certainty? The only certainty is that the phenomena are enormously complex, especially if one includes in them such intellectual flights of mediumship as Swedenborg's, and if one tries in any way to work the physical phenomena in. That is why I personally am as yet neither a convinced believer in parasitic demons, nor a spiritist, nor a scientist, but still remain a psychical researcher waiting for more facts before concluding.

Out of my experience, such as it is (and it is limited enough) one fixed conclusion dogmatically emerges, and that is this, that we with our lives are like islands in the sea, or like trees in the forest. The maple and the pine may whisper to each other with their leaves, and Conanicut and Newport hear each other's foghorns. But the trees also commingle their roots in the darkness underground, and the islands also hang together through the ocean's bottom. Just so there is a continuum of cosmic consciousness, against which our individuality builds but accidental fences, and into which our several minds plunge as into a mother-sea or reservoir. Our "normal" consciousness is circumscribed for adaptation to our external earthly environment, but the fence is weak in spots, and fitful influences from beyond leak in, showing the otherwise unverifiable common connection. Not only psychic research, but metaphysical philosophy, and speculative biology are led in their own ways to look with favor on some such "panpsychic" view of the universe as this. Assuming this common reservoir of consciousness to exist, this bank upon which we all draw, and in which so many of earth's memories must in some way be stored, or mediums would not get at them as they do, the question is, What is its own structure? What is its inner topography? This question, first squarely formulated by Myers, deserves to be called "Myers' problem" by scientific men hereafter. What are the conditions of individuation or insulation in this mother-sea? To what tracts, to what active systems functioning separately in it, do personalities correspond? Are individual "spirits" constituted there? How numerous, and of how many hierarchic orders may these then be? How permanent? How transient? And how confluent with one another may they become?

What again, are the relations between the cosmic consciousness and matter? Are there subtler forms of matter which upon occasion may enter into functional connection with the individuations in the psychic sea, and then, and then only, show themselves? — So that our ordinary human experience, on its material as well as on its mental side, would appear to be only an extract from the larger psycho-physical world?

Vast, indeed, and difficult is the inquirer's prospect here, and the most significant data for his purpose will probably be just these dingy little mediumistic facts which the Huxleyan minds of our time find so unworthy of their attention. But when was not the science of the future stirred to its conquering activities by the little rebellious exceptions to the science of the present? Hardly, as yet, has the surface of the facts called "psychic" begun to be scratched for scientific purposes. It is through following these facts, I am persuaded, that the greatest scientific conquests of the coming generation will be achieved. *Kühn ist das Mühen, herrlich der Lohn!*

IX

ON SOME MENTAL EFFECTS OF
THE EARTHQUAKE

IX

ON SOME MENTAL EFFECTS OF THE EARTHQUAKE[1]

WHEN I departed from Harvard for Stanford University last December, almost the last good-by I got was that of my old Californian friend B: "I hope they'll give you a touch of earthquake while you're there, so that you may also become acquainted with *that* Californian institution."

Accordingly, when, lying awake at about half past five on the morning of April 18 in my little "flat" on the campus of Stanford, I felt the bed begin to waggle, my first consciousness was one of gleeful recognition of the nature of the movement. "By Jove," I said to myself, "here's B'ssold earthquake,

---

[1] At the time of the San Francisco earthquake the author was at Leland Stanford University nearby. He succeeded in getting into San Francisco on the morning of the earthquake, and spent the remainder of the day in the city. These observations appeared in the *Youth's Companion* for June 7, 1906.

after all!" And then, as it went *crescendo*, "And a jolly good one it is, too!" I said.

Sitting up involuntarily, and taking a kneeling position, I was thrown down on my face as it went *fortior* shaking the room exactly as a terrier shakes a rat. Then everything that was on anything else slid off to the floor, over went bureau and chiffonier with a crash, as the *fortissimo* was reached; plaster cracked, an awful roaring noise seemed to fill the outer air, and in an instant all was still again, save the soft babble of human voices from far and near that soon began to make itself heard, as the inhabitants in costumes *negligés* in various degrees sought the greater safety of the street and yielded to the passionate desire for sympathetic communication.

The thing was over, as I understand the Lick Observatory to have declared, in forty-eight seconds. To me it felt as if about that length of time, although I have heard others say that it seemed to them longer. In my case, sensation and emotion were so strong that little thought, and no reflection or volition, were possible in the short time consumed by the phenomenon.

The emotion consisted wholly of glee and admiration; glee at the vividness which such an abstract idea or verbal term as "earthquake" could put on when translated into sensible reality and verified concretely; and admiration at the way in which the frail little wooden house could hold itself together in spite of such a shaking. I felt no trace whatever of fear; it was pure delight and welcome.

"*Go* it," I almost cried aloud, "and go it *stronger!*"

I ran into my wife's room, and found that she, although awakened from sound sleep, had felt no fear, either. Of all the persons whom I later interrogated, very few had felt any fear while the shaking lasted, although many had had a "turn," as they realized their narrow escapes from bookcases or bricks from chimney-breasts falling on their beds and pillows an instant after they had left them.

As soon as I could think, I discerned retrospectively certain peculiar ways in which my consciousness had taken in the phenomenon. These ways were quite spontaneous, and, so to speak, inevitable and irresistible.

First, I personified the earthquake as a permanent individual entity. It was *the* earthquake of my friend B's augury, which had been lying low and holding itself back during all the intervening months, in order, on that lustrous April morning, to invade my room, and energize the more intensely and triumphantly. It came, moreover, directly to *me*. It stole in behind my back, and once inside the room, had me all to itself, and could manifest itself convincingly. Animus and intent were never more present in any human action, nor did any human activity ever more definitely point back to a living agent as its source and origin.

All whom I consulted on the point agreed as to this feature in their experience. "It expressed intention," "It was vicious," "It was bent on destruction," "It wanted to show its power," or what not. To me, it wanted simply to manifest the full meaning of its *name*. But what was this "It"? To some, apparently, a vague demonic power; to me an individualized being, B's earthquake, namely.

One informant interpreted it as the end of the world and the beginning of the final judgment. This was a lady in a San Francisco hotel, who did not think of its being an earthquake till after she had got into the street and some one had explained it to her. She told me that the theological interpretation had kept fear from her mind, and made her take the shaking calmly. For "science," when the tensions in the earth's crust reach the breaking-point, and strata fall into an altered equilibrium, earthquake is simply the collective *name* of all the cracks and shakings and disturbances that happen. They *are* the earthquake. But for me *the* earthquake was the *cause* of the disturbances, and the perception of it as a living agent was irresistible. It had an overpowering dramatic convincingness.

I realize now better than ever how inevitable were men's earlier mythologic versions of such catastrophes, and how artificial and against the grain of our spontaneous perceiving are the later habits into which science educates us. It was simply impossible for untutored men to take earthquakes into their minds as anything but supernatural warnings or retributions.

A good instance of the way in which the tremendousness of a catastrophe may banish fear was given me by a Stanford student. He was in the fourth story of Encina Hall, an immense stone dormitory building. Awakened from sleep, he recognized what the disturbance was, and sprang from the bed, but was thrown off his feet in a moment, while his books and furniture fell round him. Then, with an awful, sinister, grinding roar, everything gave way, and with chimneys, floor-beams, walls and all, he descended through the three lower stories of the building into the basement. "This is my end, this is my death," he felt; but all the while no trace of fear.

The experience was too overwhelming for anything but passive surrender to it. (Certain heavy chimneys had fallen in, carrying the whole centre of the building with them.)

Arrived at the bottom, he found himself with rafters and *débris* round him, but not pinned in or crushed. He saw daylight, and crept toward it through the obstacles. Then, realizing that he was in his nightgown, and feeling no pain anywhere, his first thought was to get back to his room and find some more presentable clothing. The stairways at Encina Hall are at the ends of the building. He made his way to one of them, and went up the four flights, only to find his room no longer extant. Then he noticed pain in his feet, which had been injured, and came down the stairs with difficulty. When he talked with me ten days later he had been in hospital a week, was very thin and pale, and went on crutches, and was dressed in borrowed clothing.

So much for Stanford, where all our experiences seem to have been very similar. Nearly all our chimneys went down, some of them disintegrating from top to bottom; parlor floors were covered with bricks; plaster strewed the floors; furniture was everywhere upset and dislocated; but the wooden dwellings sprang back to their original position, and in house after house not a window stuck or a door scraped at top or bottom. Wood architecture was triumphant! Everybody was excited, but the excitement at first, at any rate, seemed to be almost joyous. Here at last was a *real* earthquake after so many years of harmless waggle! Above all, there was an irresistible desire to talk about it, and exchange experiences.

Most people slept outdoors for several subsequent nights, partly to be safer in case of a recurrence, but also to work off their emotion, and get the full unusualness out of the experience. The vocal babble of early-waking girls and boys from the gardens of the campus, mingling with the birds' songs and the exquisite weather, was for three or four days a delightful sunrise phenomenon.

Now turn to San Francisco, thirty-five miles distant, from which an automobile ere long brought us the dire news of a city in ruins, with fires beginning at various points, and the water-supply interrupted. I was fortunate enough to board the only train of cars — a very small one — that got up to the city; fortunate enough also to escape in the evening by the only train that left it. This gave me and my valiant feminine escort some four hours of observation. My business is with "subjective" phenomena exclusively; so I will say nothing of the material ruin that greeted us on every hand — the daily papers and the weekly journals have done full justice to that topic. By midday, when we reached the city, the pall of smoke was vast and the dynamite detonations had begun, but the troops, the police and the firemen seemed to have established order, dangerous neighborhoods were roped off everywhere and picketed, saloons closed, vehicles impressed, and every one at work who *could* work.

It was indeed a strange sight to see an entire

population in the streets, busy as ants in an uncovered ant-hill scurrying to save their eggs and larvæ. Every horse, and everything on wheels in the city, from hucksters' wagons to automobiles, was being loaded with what effects could be scraped together from houses which the advancing flames were threatening. The sidewalks were covered with well-dressed men and women, carrying baskets, bundles, valises, or dragging trunks to spots of greater temporary safety, soon to be dragged farther, as the fire kept spreading!

In the safer quarters, every doorstep was covered with the dwelling's tenants, sitting surrounded with their more indispensable chattels, and ready to flee at a minute's notice. I think every one must have fasted on that day, for I saw no one eating. There was no appearance of general dismay, and little of chatter or of inco-ordinated excitement.

Every one seemed doggedly bent on achieving the job which he had set himself to perform; and the faces, although somewhat tense and set and grave, were inexpressive of

emotion. I noticed only three persons overcome, two Italian women, very poor, embrac-
ing an aged fellow countrywoman, and all
weeping. Physical fatigue and *seriousness*
were the only inner states that one could
read on countenances.

With lights forbidden in the houses, and the
streets lighted only by the conflagration, it was
apprehended that the criminals of San Francisco would hold high carnival on the ensuing
night. But whether they feared the disciplinary methods of the United States troops,
who were visible everywhere, or whether
they were themselves solemnized by the immensity of the disaster, they lay low and did
not "manifest," either then or subsequently.

The only very discreditable thing to human
nature that occurred was later, when hundreds
of lazy "bummers" found that they could
keep camping in the parks, and make alimen-
tary storage-batteries of their stomachs, even
in some cases getting enough of the free rations
in their huts or tents to last them well into the
summer. This charm of pauperized vaga-

bondage seems all along to have been Satan's most serious bait to human nature. There was theft from the outset, but confined, I believe, to petty pilfering.

Cash in hand was the only money, and millionaires and their families were no better off in this respect than any one. Whoever got a vehicle could have the use of it; but the richest often went without, and spent the first two nights on rugs on the bare ground, with nothing but what their own arms had rescued. Fortunately, those nights were dry and comparatively warm, and Californians are accustomed to camping conditions in the summer, so suffering from exposure was less great than it would have been elsewhere. By the fourth night, which was rainy, tents and huts had brought most campers under cover.

I went through the city again eight days later. The fire was out, and about a quarter of the area stood unconsumed. Intact skyscrapers dominated the smoking level majestically and superbly — they and a few walls that had survived the overthrow. Thus has the courage of our architects and builders received triumphant vindication!

The inert elements of the population had mostly got away, and those that remained seemed what Mr. H. G. Wells calls "efficients." Sheds were already going up as temporary starting-points of business. Every one looked cheerful, in spite of the awful discontinuity of past and future, with every familiar asso-ciation with material things dissevered; and the discipline and order were practically perfect.

As these notes of mine must be short, I had better turn to my more generalized reflections.

Two things in retrospect strike me espe-cially, and are the most emphatic of all my impressions. Both are reassuring as to human nature.

The first of these was the rapidity of the improvisation of order out of chaos. It is clear that just as in every thousand human beings there will be statistically so many artists, so many athletes, so many thinkers,

and so many potentially good soldiers, so
there will be so many potential organizers in
times of emergency. In point of fact, not
only in the great city, but in the outlying
towns, these natural ordermakers, whether
amateurs or officials, came to the front immediately. There seemed to be no possibility which there was not some one there to
think of, or which within twenty-four hours
was not in some way provided for.

A good illustration is this: Mr. Keith is the
great landscape-painter of the Pacific slope,
and his pictures, which are many, are artistic-
ally and pecuniarily precious. Two citizens,
lovers of his work, early in the day diverted
their attention from all other interests, their
own private ones included, and made it their
duty to visit every place which they knew to
contain a Keith painting. They cut them from
their frames, rolled them up, and in this way
got all the more important ones into a place
of safety.

When they then sought Mr. Keith, to convey the joyous news to him, they found him

still in his studio, which was remote from the fire, beginning a new painting. Having given up his previous work for lost, he had resolved to lose no time in making what amends he could for the disaster.

The completeness of organization at Palo Alto, a town of ten thousand inhabitants close to Stanford University, was almost comical. People feared exodus on a large scale of the rowdy elements of San Francisco. In point of fact, very few refugees came to Palo Alto. But within twenty-four hours, rations, clothing, hospital, quarantine, disinfection, washing, police, military, quarters in camp and in houses, printed information, employment, all were provided for under the care of so many volunteer committees.

Much of this readiness was American, much of it Californian; but I believe that every country in a similar crisis would have displayed it in a way to astonish the spectators. Like soldiering, it lies always latent in human nature.

The second thing that struck me was the

universal equanimity. We soon got letters
from the East, ringing with anxiety and
pathos; but I now know fully what I have
always believed, that the pathetic way of feeling great disasters belongs rather to the point
of view of people at a distance than to the
immediate victims. I heard not a single
really pathetic or sentimental word in California expressed by any one.

The terms "awful," "dreadful" fell often
enough from people's lips, but always with a
sort of abstract meaning, and with a face that
seemed to admire the vastness of the catastrophe as much as it bewailed its cuttingness.
When talk was not directly practical, I might
almost say that it expressed (at any rate
in the nine days I was there) a tendency
more toward nervous excitement than toward
grief. The hearts concealed private bitterness
enough, no doubt, but the tongues disdained to
dwell on the misfortunes of self, when almost
everybody one spoke to had suffered equally.

Surely the cutting edge of all our usual
misfortunes comes from their character of

loneliness. We lose our health, our wife or children die, our house burns down, or our money is made way with, and the world goes on rejoicing, leaving us on one side and counting us out from all its business. In California every one, to some degree, was suffering, and one's private miseries were merged in the vast general sum of privation and in the all-absorbing practical problem of general recuperation. The cheerfulness, or, at any rate, the steadfastness of tone, was universal. Not a single whine or plaintive word did I hear from the hundred losers whom I spoke to. Instead of that there was a temper of helpfulness beyond the counting.

It is easy to glorify this as something characteristically American, or especially Californian. Californian education has, of course, made the thought of all possible recuperations easy. In an exhausted country, with no marginal resources, the outlook on the future would be much darker. But I like to think that what I write of is a normal and universal trait of human nature. In our drawing-rooms and offices we wonder how people ever *do* go through battles, sieges and shipwrecks. We quiver and sicken in imagination, and think those heroes superhuman. Physical pain, whether suffered alone or in company, is always more or less unnerving and intolerable. But mental pathos and anguish, I fancy, are usually effects of distance. At the place of action, where all are concerned together, healthy animal insensibility and heartiness take their place. At San Francisco the need will continue to be awful, and there will doubtless be a crop of nervous wrecks before the weeks and months are over, but meanwhile the commonest men, simply because they *are* men, will go on, singly and collectively, showing this admirable fortitude of temper.

X

THE ENERGIES OF MEN

X

THE ENERGIES OF MEN[1]

Everyone knows what it is to start a piece of work, either intellectual or muscular, feeling stale — or *oold*, as an Adirondack guide once put it to me. And everybody knows what it is to "warm up" to his job. The process of warming up gets particularly striking in the phenomenon known as "second wind." On usual occasions we make a practice of stopping an occupation as soon as we meet the first effective layer (so to call it) of fatigue. We have then walked, played, or worked "enough," so we desist. That amount of fatigue is an efficacious obstruction on this

[1] This was the title originally given to the Presidential Address delivered before the American Philosophical Association at Columbia University, December 28, 1906, and published as there delivered in the *Philosophical Review* for January, 1907. The address was later published, after slight alteration, in the *American Magazine* for October, 1907, under the title "The Powers of Men." The more popular form is here reprinted under the title which the author himself preferred.

side of which our usual life is cast. But if an unusual necessity forces us to press onward, a surprising thing occurs. The fatigue gets worse up to a certain critical point, when gradually or suddenly it passes away, and we are fresher than before. We have evidently tapped a level of new energy, masked until then by the fatigue-obstacle usually obeyed. There may be layer after layer of this experience. A third and a fourth "wind" may supervene. Mental activity shows the phenomenon as well as physical, and in exceptional cases we may find, beyond the very extremity of fatigue-distress, amounts of ease and power that we never dreamed ourselves to own, — sources of strength habitually not taxed at all, because habitually we never push through the obstruction, never pass those early critical points.

For many years I have mused on the phenomenon of second wind, trying to find a physiological theory. It is evident that our organism has stored-up reserves of energy that are ordinarily not called upon, but that may be called upon: deeper and deeper strata of combustible or explosible material, discontinuously arranged, but ready for use by anyone who probes so deep, and repairing themselves by rest as well as do the superficial strata. Most of us continue living unnecessarily near our surface. Our energy-budget is like our nutritive budget. Physiologists say that a man is in "nutritive equilibrium" when day after day he neither gains nor loses weight. But the odd thing is that this condition may obtain on astonishingly different amounts of food. Take a man in nutritive equilibrium, and systematically increase or lessen his rations. In the first case he will begin to gain weight, in the second case to lose it. The change will be greatest on the first day, less on the second, less still on the third; and so on, till he has gained all that he will gain, or lost all that he will lose, on that altered diet. He is now in nutritive equilibrium again, but with a new weight; and this neither lessens nor increases because his various combustion-processes have adjusted themselves to the changed dietary. He gets rid, in one way or another, of just as much N, C, H, etc., as he takes in *per diem*.

Just so one can be in what I might call "efficiency-equilibrium" (neither gaining nor losing power when once the equilibrium is reached) on astonishingly different quantities of work, no matter in what direction the work may be measured. It may be physical work, intellectual work, moral work, or spiritual work.

Of course there are limits: the trees don't grow into the sky. But the plain fact remains that men the world over possess amounts of resource which only very exceptional individuals push to their extremes of use. But the very same individual, pushing his energies to their extreme, may in a vast number of cases keep the pace up day after day, and find no "reaction" of a bad sort, so long as decent hygienic conditions are preserved. His more active rate of energizing does not wreck him; for the organism adapts itself, and as the rate of waste augments,

augments correspondingly the rate of re-pair.

I say the *rate* and not the *time* of repair. The busiest man needs no more hours of rest than the idler. Some years ago Professor Patrick, of the Iowa State University, kept three young men awake for four days and nights. When his observations on them were finished, the subjects were permitted to sleep themselves out. All awoke from this sleep completely refreshed, but the one who took longest to restore himself from his long vigil only slept one-third more time than was regular with him.

If my reader will put together these two conceptions, first, that few men live at their maximum of energy, and second, that anyone may be in vital equilibrium at very different rates of energizing, he will find, I think, that a very pretty practical problem of national economy, as well as of individual ethics, opens upon his view. In rough terms, we may say that a man who energizes below his normal maximum fails by just so much to profit by his chance at life; and that a nation filled with such men is inferior to a nation run at higher pressure. The problem is, then, how can men be trained up to their most useful pitch of energy? And how can nations make such training most accessible to all their sons and daughters. This, after all, is only the general problem of education, formulated in slightly different terms.

"Rough" terms, I said just now, because the words "energy" and "maximum" may easily suggest only *quantity* to the reader's mind, whereas in measuring the human energies of which I speak, qualities as well as quantities have to be taken into account. Everyone feels that his total *power* rises when he passes to a higher *qualitative* level of life.

Writing is higher than walking, thinking is higher than writing, deciding higher than thinking, deciding "no" higher than deciding "yes" — at least the man who passes from one of these activities to another will usually say that each later one involves a greater element of *inner work* than the earlier ones, even though the total heat given out or the foot-pounds expended by the organism, may be less. Just how to conceive this inner work physiologically is as yet impossible, but psychologically we all know what the word means. We need a particular spur or effort to start us upon inner work; it tires us to sustain it; and when long sustained, we know how easily we lapse. When I speak of "energizing," and its rates and levels and sources, I mean therefore our inner as well as our outer work.

Let no one think, then, that our problem of individual and national economy is solely that of the maximum of pounds raisable against gravity, the maximum of locomotion, or of agitation of any sort, that human beings can accomplish. That might signify little more than hurrying and jumping about in inco-ordinated ways; whereas inner work, though it so often reinforces outer work, quite as often means its arrest. To relax, to say to ourselves (with the "new thought-ers") "Peace! be still!" is sometimes a great achievement of inner work. When I speak of human energizing in general, the reader must therefore understand that sum-total of activities, some outer and some inner, some muscular, some emotional, some moral, some spiritual, of whose waxing and waning in himself he is at all times so well aware. How to keep it at an appreciable maximum? How not to let the level lapse? That is the great problem. But the work of men and women is of innumerable kinds, each kind being, as we say, carrried on by a particular faculty; so the great problem splits into two sub-problems, thus:

(1). What are the limits of human faculty in various directions?

(2). By what diversity of means, in the differing types of human beings, may the faculties be stimulated to their best results?

Read in one way, these two questions sound both trivial and familiar: there is a sense in which we have all asked them ever since we were born. Yet *as a methodical programme of scientific inquiry*, I doubt whether they have ever been seriously taken up. If answered

236

fully, almost the whole of mental science and of the science of conduct would find a place under them. I propose, in what follows, to press them on the reader's attention in an informal way.

The first point to agree upon in this enterprise is that *as a rule men habitually use only a small part of the powers which they actually possess and which they might use under appropriate conditions.*

Every one is familiar with the phenomenon of feeling more or less alive on different days. Every one knows on any given day that there are energies slumbering in him which the incitements of that day do not call forth, but which he might display if these were greater. Most of us feel as if a sort of cloud weighed upon us, keeping us below our highest notch of clearness in discernment, sureness in reasoning, or firmness in deciding. Compared with what we ought to be, we are only half awake. Our fires are damped, our drafts are checked. We are making use of only a small part of our possible mental and physical resources. In some persons this sense of being cut off from their rightful resources is extreme, and we then get the formidable neurasthenic and psychasthenic conditions, with life grown into one tissue of impossibilities, that so many medical books decribe.

Stating the thing broadly, the human individual thus lives usually far within his limits; he possesses powers of various sorts which he habitually fails to use. He energizes below his *maximum*, and he behaves below his *optimum*. In elementary faculty, in co-ordination, in power of *inhibition* and control, in every conceivable way, his life is contracted like the field of vision of an hysteric subject — but with less excuse, for the poor hysteric is diseased, while in the rest of us it is only an inveterate *habit* — the habit of inferiority to our full self — that is bad.

Admit so much, then, and admit also that the charge of being inferior to their full self is far truer of some men than of others; then the practical question ensues: *to what do the better men owe their escape? and, in the fluc-*

238

tuations which all men feel in their own degree of energizing, to what are the improvements due, when they occur?

In general terms the answer is plain:

Either some unusual stimulus fills them with emotional excitement, or some unusual idea of necessity induces them to make an extra effort of will. *Excitements, ideas, and efforts,* in a word, are what carry us over the dam.

In those "hyperesthetic" conditions which chronic invalidism so often brings in its train, the dam has changed its normal place. The slightest functional exercise gives a distress which the patient yields to and stops. In such cases of "habit-neurosis" a new range of power often comes in consequence of the "bullying-treatment," of efforts which the doctor obliges the patient, much against his will, to make. First comes the very extremity of distress, then follows unexpected relief. There seems no doubt that *we are each and all of us to some extent victims of habit-neurosis.* We have to admit the wider potential range and the habitually narrow actual use. We

239

live subject to arrest by degrees of fatigue which we have come only from habit to obey. Most of us may learn to push the barrier farther off, and to live in perfect comfort on much higher levels of power.

Country people and city people, as a class, illustrate this difference. The rapid rate of life, the number of decisions in an hour, the many things to keep account of, in a busy city man's or woman's life, seem monstrous to a country brother. He does n't see how we live at all. A day in New York or Chicago fills him with terror. The danger and noise make it appear like a permanent earthquake. But *settle* him there, and in a year or two he will have caught the pulse-beat. He will vibrate to the city's rhythms; and if he only succeeds in his avocation, whatever that may be, he will find a joy in all the hurry and the tension, he will keep the pace as well as any of us, and get as much out of himself in any week as he ever did in ten weeks in the country.

The stimuli of those who successfully respond and undergo the transformation here, are duty, the example of others, and crowd-pressure and contagion. The transformation, moreover, is a chronic one: the new level of energy becomes permanent. The duties of new offices of trust are constantly producing this effect on the human beings appointed to them. The physiologists call a stimulus "dynamogenic" when it increases the muscular contractions of men to whom it is applied; but appeals can be dynamogenic morally as well as muscularly. We are witnessing here in America to-day the dynamogenic effect of a very exalted political office upon the energies of an individual who had already manifested a healthy amount of energy before the office came.

Humbler examples show perhaps still better what chronic effects duty's appeal may produce in chosen individuals. John Stuart Mill somewhere says that women excel men in the power of keeping up sustained moral excitement. Every case of illness nursed by wife or mother is a proof of this; and where can one find greater examples of sustained endurance than in those thousands of poor homes, where the woman successfully holds the family together and keeps it going by taking all the thought and doing all the work – nursing, teaching, cooking, washing, sewing, scrubbing, saving, helping neighbors, "choring" outside — where does the catalogue end? If she does a bit of scolding now and then who can blame her? But often she does just the reverse; keeping the children clean and the man good tempered, and soothing and smoothing the whole neighborhood into finer shape.

Eighty years ago a certain Montyon left to the Académie Française a sum of money to be given in small prizes, to the best examples of "virtue" of the year. The academy's committees, with great good sense, have shown a partiality to virtues simple and chronic, rather than to her spasmodic and dramatic flights; and the exemplary housewives reported on have been wonderful and admirable enough. In Paul Bourget's report for this year we find numerous cases, of which this is a type; Jeanne Chaix, eldest of six children; mother insane, father chronically ill. Jeanne, with no money but her wages at a pasteboard-box factory, directs the household, brings up the children, and successfully maintains the family of eight, which thus subsists, morally as well as materially, by the sole force of her valiant will. In some of these French cases charity to outsiders is added to the inner family burden; or helpless relatives, young or old, are adopted, as if the strength were inexhaustible and ample for every appeal. Details are too long to quote here; but human nature, responding to the call of duty, appears nowhere sublimer than in the person of these humble heroines of family life.

Turning from more chronic to acuter proofs of human nature's reserves of power, we find that the stimuli that carry us over the usually effective dam are most often the classic emotional ones, love, anger, crowd-contagion or despair. Despair lames most people, but it

wakes others fully up. Every siege or shipwreck or polar expedition brings out some
hero who keeps the whole company in heart.
Last year there was a terrible colliery explosion at Courrieres in France. Two hundred
corpses, if I remember rightly, were exhumed.
After twenty days of excavation, the rescuers
heard a voice. "*Me voici*," said the first
man unearthed. He proved to be a collier
named Nemy, who had taken command of
thirteen others in the darkness, disciplined
them and cheered them, and brought them
out alive. Hardly any of them could see or
speak or walk when brought into the day.
Five days later, a different type of vital endurance was unexpectedly unburied in the
person of one Berton who, isolated from any
but dead companions, had been able to sleep
away most of his time.

A new position of responsibility will usually
show a man to be a far stronger creature than
was supposed. Cromwell's and Grant's ca-
reers are the stock examples of how war will
wake a man up. I owe to Professor C. E.

Norton, my colleague, the permission to print part of a private letter from Colonel Baird-Smith written shortly after the six weeks' siege of Delhi, in 1857, for the victorious issue of which that excellent officer was chiefly to be thanked. He writes as follows:

" . . . My poor wife had some reason to think that war and disease between them had left very little of a husband to take under nursing when she got him again. An attack of camp-scurvy had filled my mouth with sores, shaken every joint in my body, and covered me all over with sores and livid spots, so that I was marvellously unlovely to look upon. A smart knock on the ankle-joint from the splinter of a shell that burst in my face, in itself a mere *bagatelle* of a wound, had been of necessity neglected under the pressing and incessant calls upon me, and had grown worse and worse till the whole foot below the ankle became a black mass and seemed to threaten mortification. I insisted, however, on being allowed to use it till the place was taken, mortification or no; and though the pain was sometimes horrible, I carried my point and kept up to the last. On the day after the assault I had an unlucky fall on some bad ground, and it was an open question for a day or two whether I hadn't broken my arm at the elbow. Fortunately it turned out to be only a severe sprain, but I am still conscious of the wrench it gave me. To crown the whole pleasant catalogue, I was worn to a shadow by a constant diarrhœa, and consumed as much opium as would have done credit to my father-in-law [Thomas De Quincey]. However, thank God, I have a good share of Tapleyism in me and come out strong under difficulties. I think I may confidently say that no man ever saw me out of heart, or ever heard one croaking word from me even when our prospects were gloomiest. We were sadly scourged by the cholera, and it was almost appalling to me to find that out of twenty-seven officers present, I could only muster fifteen for the operations of the attack. However, it was done, and

246

after it was done came the collapse. Don't be horrified when I tell you that for the whole of the actual siege, and in truth for some little time before, I almost lived on brandy. Appetite for food I had none, but I forced myself to eat just sufficient to sustain life, and I had an incessant craving for brandy as the strongest stimulant I could get. Strange to say, I was quite unconscious of its affecting me in the slightest degree. *The excitement of the work was so great that no lesser one seemed to have any chance against it, and I certainly never found my intellect clearer or my nerves stronger in my life.* It was only my wretched body that was weak, and the moment the real work was done by our becoming complete masters of Delhi, I broke down without delay and discovered that if I wished to live I must continue no longer the system that had kept me up until the crisis was passed. With it passed away as if in a moment all desire to stimulate, and a perfect loathing of my late staff of life took possession of me."

Such experiences show how profound is the

alteration in the manner in which, under excitement, our organism will sometimes perform its physiological work. The processes of repair become different when the reserves have to be used, and for weeks and months the deeper use may go on.

Morbid cases, here as elsewhere, lay the normal machinery bare. In the first number of Dr. Morton Prince's *Journal of Abnormal Psychology*, Dr. Janet has discussed five cases of morbid impulse, with an explanation that is precious for my present point of view. One is a girl who eats, eats, eats, all day. Another walks, walks, walks, and gets her food from an automobile that escorts her. Another is a dipsomaniac. A fourth pulls out her hair. A fifth wounds her flesh and burns her skin. Hitherto such freaks of impulse have received Greek names (as bulimia, dromomania, etc.) and been scientifically disposed of as "episodic syndromata of hereditary degeneration." But it turns out that Janet's cases are all what he calls psychasthenics, or victims of a chronic sense of weakness, torpor, lethargy, fatigue, insufficiency, impossibility, unreality and powerlessness of will; and that in each and all of them the particular activity pursued, deleterious though it be, has the temporary result of raising the sense of vitality and making the patient feel alive again. These things reanimate: they would reanimate *us*, but it happens that in each patient the particular freak-activity chosen is the only thing that does reanimate; and therein lies the morbid state. The way to treat such persons is to discover to them more usual and useful ways of throwing their stores of vital energy into gear.

Colonel Baird-Smith, needing to draw on altogether extraordinary stores of energy, found that brandy and opium were ways of throwing them into gear.

Such cases are humanly typical. We are all to some degree oppressed, unfree. We don't come to our own. It is there, but we don't get at it. The threshold must be made to shift. Then many of us find that an eccentric activity — a "spree," say — relieves.

There is no doubt that to some men sprees and excesses of almost any kind are medicinal, temporarily at any rate, in spite of what the moralists and doctors say.

But when the normal tasks and stimulations of life don't put a man's deeper levels of energy on tap, and he requires distinctly deleterious excitements, his constitution verges on the abnormal. The normal opener of deeper and deeper levels of energy is the will. The difficulty is to use it, to make the effort which the word volition implies. But if we *do* make it (or if a god, though he were only the god Chance, makes it through us), it will act dynamogenically on us for a month. It is notorious that a single successful effort of moral volition, such as saying "no" to some habitual temptation, or performing some courageous act, will launch a man on a higher level of energy for days and weeks, will give him a new range of power. "In the act of uncorking the whiskey bottle which I had brought home to get drunk upon," said a man to me, "I suddenly found myself running out into the garden, where I smashed it on the ground. I felt so happy and uplifted after this act, that for two months I was n't tempted to touch a drop."

The emotions and excitements due to usual situations are the usual inciters of the will. But these act discontinuously; and in the intervals the shallower levels of life tend to close in and shut us off. Accordingly the best practical knowers of the human soul have invented the thing known as methodical ascetic discipline to keep the deeper levels constantly in reach. Beginning with easy tasks, passing to harder ones, and exercising day by day, it is, I believe, admitted that disciples of asceticism can reach very high levels of freedom and power of will.

Ignatius Loyola's spiritual exercises must have produced this result in innumerable devotees. But the most venerable ascetic system, and the one whose results have the most voluminous experimental corroboration is undoubtedly the Yoga system in Hindustan. From time immemorial, by Hatha Yoga, Raja

Yoga, Karma Yoga, or whatever code of practice it might be, Hindu aspirants to perfection have trained themselves, month in and out, for years. The result claimed, and certainly in many cases accorded by impartial judges, is strength of character, personal power, unshakability of soul. In an article in the *Philosophical Review*,[1] from which I am largely copying here, I have quoted at great length the experience with "Hatha Yoga" of a very gifted European friend of mine who, by persistently carrying out for several months its methods of fasting from food and sleep, its exercises in breathing and thought-concentration, and its fantastic posture-gymnastics, seems to have succeeded in waking up deeper and deeper levels of will and moral and intellectual power in himself, and to have escaped from a decidedly menacing brain-condition of the "circular" type, from which he had suffered for years.

Judging by my friend's letters, of which the

[1] "The Energies of Men." *Philosophical Review*, vol. xvi, No.1, January, 1907. [Cf. Note on p. 229.]

last I have is written fourteen months after the Yoga training began, there can be no doubt of his relative regeneration. He has undergone material trials with indifference, travelled third-class on Mediterranean steamers, and fourth-class on African trains, living with the poorest Arabs and sharing their unaccustomed food, all with equanimity. His devotion to certain interests has been put to heavy strain, and nothing is more remarkable to me than the changed moral tone with which he reports the situation. A profound modification has unquestionably occurred in the running of his mental machinery. The gearing has changed, and his will is available otherwise than it was.

My friend is a man of very peculiar temperament. Few of us would have had the will to start upon the Yoga training, which, once started, seemed to conjure the further will-power needed out of itself. And not all of those who could launch themselves would have reached the same results. The Hindus themselves admit that in some men the results may come without call or bell. My friend writes to me: "You are quite right in thinking that religious crises, love-crises, indignation-crises may awaken in a very short time powers similar to those reached by years of patient Yoga-practice."

Probably most medical men would treat this individual's case as one of what it is fashionable now to call by the name of "self-suggestion," or "expectant attention" — as if those phrases were explanatory, or meant more than the fact that certain men can be influenced, while others cannot be influenced, by certain sorts of *ideas*. This leads me to say a word about ideas considered as dynamogenic agents, or 'stimuli for unlocking what would otherwise be unused reservoirs of individual power.

One thing that ideas do is to contradict other ideas and keep us from believing them. An idea that thus negates a first idea may itself in turn be negated by a third idea, and the first idea may thus regain its natural influence over our belief and determine our behavior. Our philosophic and religious development proceeds thus by credulities, negations, and the negating of negations.

But whether for arousing or for stopping belief, ideas may fail to be efficacious, just as a wire at one time alive with electricity, may at another time be dead. Here our insight into causes fails us, and we can only note results in general terms. In general, whether a given idea shall be a live idea depends more on the person into whose mind it is injected than on the idea itself. Which is the suggestive idea for this person, and which for that one? Mr. Fletcher's disciples regenerate themselves by the idea (and the fact) that they are chewing, and re-chewing, and super-chewing their food. Dr. Dewey's pupils regenerate themselves by going without their breakfast — a fact, but also an ascetic idea. Not every one can use *these* ideas with the same success.

But apart from such individually varying susceptibilities, there are common lines along which men simply as men tend to be inflammable by ideas. As certain objects naturally awaken love, anger, or cupidity, so certain ideas naturally awaken the energies of loyalty, courage, endurance, or devotion. When these ideas are effective in an individual's life, their effect is often very great indeed. They may transfigure it, unlocking innumerable powers which, but for the idea, would never have come into play. "Father-land," "the Flag," "the Union," "Holy Church," "the Monroe Doctrine," "Truth," "Science," "Liberty," Garibaldi's phrase, "Rome or Death," etc., are so many examples of energy-releasing ideas. The social nature of such phrases is an essential factor of their dynamic power. They are forces of detent in situations in which no other force produces equivalent effects, and each is a force of detent only in a specific group of men.

The memory that an oath or vow has been made will nerve one to abstinences and efforts otherwise impossible; witness the "pledge" in the history of the temperance movement. A mere promise to his sweetheart will clean up a youth's life all over — at any rate for a

time. For such effects an educated sus-
ceptibility is required. The idea of one's
"honor," for example, unlocks energy only
in those of us who have had the education of
a "gentleman," so called.

That delightful being, Prince Pueckler-
Muskau, writes to his wife from England that
he has invented "a sort of artificial resolution respecting things that are difficult of
performance. My device," he continues,
"is this: *I give my word of honor most solemnly
to myself* to do or to leave undone this or
that. I am of course extremely cautious in
the use of this expedient, but when once the
word is given, even though I afterwards think
I have been precipitate or mistaken, I hold
it to be perfectly irrevocable, whatever incon-
veniences I foresee likely to result. If I were
capable of brea kingmy word after such ma-
ture consideration, I should lose all respect
for myself, — and what man of sense would
not prefer death to such an alternative? . . .
When the mysterious formula is pronounced,
no alteration in my own view, nothing short

of physical impossibilities, must, for the welfare of my soul, alter my will. . . . I find something very satisfactory in the thought that man has the power of framing such props and weapons out of the most trivial materials, indeed out of nothing, merely by the force of his will, which thereby truly deserves the name of omnipotent." [1]

Conversions, whether they be political, scientific, philosophic, or religious, form another way in which bound energies are let loose. They unify us, and put a stop to ancient mental interferences. The result is freedom, and often a great enlargement of power. A belief that thus settles upon an individual always acts as a challenge to his will. But, for the particular challenge to operate, he must be the right challeng*ee*. In religious conversions we have so fine an adjustment that the idea may be in the mind of the challengee for years before it exerts effects; and why it should do so then is often so far from

[1] "Tour in England, Ireland, and France," Philadelphia, 1833, p. 435.

obvious that the event is taken for a miracle of grace, and not a natural occurrence. Whatever it is, it may be a highwater mark of energy, in which "noes," once impossible, are easy, and in which a new range of "yeses" gains the right of way.

We are just now witnessing a very copious unlocking of energies by ideas in the persons of those converts to "New Thought," "Christian Science," "Metaphysical Healing," or other forms of spiritual philosophy, who are so numerous among us to-day. The ideas here are healthy-minded and optimistic; and it is quite obvious that a wave of religious activity, analogous in some respects to the spread of early Christianity, Buddhism, and Mohammedanism, is passing over our American world. The common feature of these optimistic faiths is that they all tend to the suppression of what Mr. Horace Fletcher calls "fearthought." Fearthought he defines as the "self-suggestion of inferiority"; so that one may say that these systems all operate by the suggestion of power. And the power, small or great, comes in various shapes to the individual, — power, as he will tell you, not to "mind" things that used to vex him, power to concentrate his mind, good cheer, good temper — in short, to put it mildly, a firmer, more elastic moral tone.

The most genuinely saintly person I have ever known is a friend of mine now suffering from cancer of the breast — I hope that she may pardon my citing her here as an example of what ideas can do. Her ideas have kept her a practically well woman for months after she should have given up and gone to bed. They have annulled all pain and weakness and given her a cheerful active life, unusually beneficent to others to whom she has afforded help. Her doctors, acquiescing in results they could not understand, have had the good sense to let her go her own way.

How far the mind-cure movement is destined to extend its influence, or what intellectual modifications it may yet undergo, no one can foretell. It is essentially a religious movement, and to academically nurtured minds its utterances are tasteless and often grotesque enough. It also incurs the natural enmity of medical politicians, and of the whole trades-union wing of that profession. But no unprejudiced observer can fail to recognize its importance as a social phenomenon to-day, and the higher medical minds are already trying to interpret it fairly, and make its power available for their own therapeutic ends.

Dr. Thomas Hyslop, of the great West Riding Asylum in England, said last year to the British Medical Association that the best sleep-producing agent which his practice had revealed to him, was *prayer*. I say this, he added (I am sorry here that I must quote from memory), purely as a medical man. The exercise of prayer, in those who habitually exert it, must be regarded by us doctors as the most adequate and normal of all the pacifiers of the mind and calmers of the nerves.

But in few of us are functions not tied up by the exercise of other functions. Relatively few medical men and scientific men, I fancy,

261

can pray. Few can carry on any living commerce with "God." Yet many of us are well aware of how much freer and abler our lives would be, were such important forms of energizing not sealed up by the critical atmosphere in which we have been reared. There are in every one potential forms of activity that actually are shunted out from use. Part of the imperfect vitality under which we labor can thus be easily explained. One part of our mind dams up — even *damns* up! — the other parts.

Conscience makes cowards of us all. Social conventions prevent us from telling the truth after the fashion of the heroes and heroines of Bernard Shaw. We all know persons who are models of excellence, but who belong to the extreme philistine type of mind. So deadly is their intellectual respectability that we can't converse about certain subjects at all, can't let our our minds play over them, can't even mention them in their presence. I have numbered among my dearest friends persons thus inhibited intellectually, with whom I would gladly have been able to talk freely about certain interests of mine, certain authors, say, as Bernard Shaw, Chesterton, Edward Carpenter, H. G. Wells, but it would n't do, it made them too uncomfortable, they would n't play, I had to be silent. An intellect thus tied down by literality and decorum makes on one the same sort of an impression that an able-bodied man would who should habituate himself to do his work with only one of his fingers, locking up the rest of his organism and leaving it unused.

I trust that by this time I have said enough to convince the reader both of the truth and of the importance of my thesis. The two questions, first, that of the possible extent of our powers; and, second, that of the various avenues of approach to them, the various keys for unlocking them in diverse individuals, dominate the whole problem of individual and national education. We need a topography of the limits of human power, similar to the chart which oculists use of the field of human vision. We need also a study of the various types of human being with reference to the different ways in which their energy-reserves may be appealed to and set loose. Biographies and individual experiences of every kind may be drawn upon for evidence here. [1]

[1] " This would be an absolutely concrete study . . . The limits of power must be limits that have been realized in actual persons, and the various ways of unlocking the reserves of power must have been exemplified in individual lives . . . So here is a program of concrete individual psychology . . . It is replete with interesting facts, and points to practical issues superior in importance to anything we know." *From the address as originally delivered before the Philosophical Association;* See xvi. *Philosophical Review,* 1, 19.

XI

THE MORAL EQUIVALENT OF WAR

XI

THE MORAL EQUIVALENT OF WAR[1]

The war against war is going to be no holiday excursion or camping party. The military feelings are too deeply grounded to abdicate their place among our ideals until better substitutes are offered than the glory and shame that come to nations as well as to individuals from the ups and downs of politics and the vicissitudes of trade. There is something highly paradoxical in the modern man's relation to war. Ask all our millions, north and south, whether they would vote now (were such a thing possible) to have our war for the Union expunged from history, and the record of a peaceful transition to the present time substituted for that of its marches and battles, and probably hardly a handful of eccentrics would say yes. Those

---

[1] Written for and first published by the Association for International Conciliation (Leaflet No. 27) and also published in *McClure's Magazine*, August, 1910, and *The Popular Science Monthly*, October, 1910.

ancestors, those efforts, those memories and legends, are the most ideal part of what we now own together, a sacred spiritual possession worth more than all the blood poured out. Yet ask those same people whether they would be willing in cold blood to start another civil war now to gain another similar possession, and not one man or women would vote for the proposition. In modern eyes, precious though wars may be, they must not be waged solely for the sake of the ideal harvest. Only when forced upon one, only when an enemy's injustice leaves us no alternative, is a war now thought permissible.

It was not thus in ancient times. The earlier men were hunting men, and to hunt a neighboring tribe, kill the males, loot the village and possess the females, was the most profitable, as well as the most exciting, way of living. Thus were the more martial tribes selected, and in chiefs and peoples a pure pugnacity and love of glory came to mingle with the more fundamental appetite for plunder.

Modern war is so expensive that we feel trade to be a better avenue to plunder; but modern man inherits all the innate pugnacity and all the love of glory of his ancestors. Showing war's irrationality and horror is of no effect upon him. The horrors make the fascination. War is the *strong* life; it is life *in extremis;* war-taxes are the only ones men never hesitate to pay, as the budgets of all nations show us.

History is a bath of blood. The Iliad is one long recital of how Diomedes and Ajax, Sarpedon and Hector *killed.* No detail of the wounds they made is spared us, and the Greek mind fed upon the story. Greek history is a panorama of jingoism and imperialism — war for war's sake, all the citizens being warriors. It is horrible reading, because of the irrationality of it all — save for the purpose of making "history" — and the history is that of the utter ruin of a civilization in intellectual respects perhaps the highest the earth has ever seen.

Those wars were purely piratical. Pride,

gold, women, slaves, excitement, were their
only motives. In the Peloponnesian war for
example, the Athenians ask the inhabitants of
Melos (the island where the "Venus of Milo"
was found), hitherto neutral, to own their
lordship. The envoys meet, and hold a debate
which Thucydides gives in full, and which, for
sweet reasonableness of form, would have satisfied Matthew Arnold. "The powerful exact
what they can," said the Athenians, "and the
weak grant what they must." When the Meleans say that sooner than be slaves they will
appeal to the gods, the Athenians reply: "Of
the gods we believe and of men we know that,
by a law of their nature, wherever they can
rule they will. This law was not made by us,
and we are not the first to have acted upon it;
we did but inherit it, and we know that you
and all mankind, if you were as strong as we
are, would do as we do. So much for the gods;
we have told you why we expect to stand as
high in their good opinion as you." Well, the
Meleans still refused, and their town was
taken. "The Athenians," Thucydides quietly

says, "thereupon put to death all who were of military age and made slaves of the women and children. They then colonized the island, sending thither five hundred settlers of their own."

Alexander's career was piracy pure and simple, nothing but an orgy of power and plunder, made romantic by the character of the hero. There was no rational principle in it, and the moment he died his generals and governors attacked one another. The cruelty of those times is incredible. When Rome finally conquered Greece, Paulus Æmilius, was told by the Roman Senate to reward his soldiers for their toil by "giving" them the old kingdom of Epirus. They sacked seventy cities and carried off a hundred and fifty thousand inhabitants as slaves. How many they killed I know not; but in Etolia they killed all the senators, five hundred and fifty in number. Brutus was "the noblest Roman of them all," but to reanimate his soldiers on the eve of Philippi he similarly promises to give them the cities of Sparta and

Thessalonica to ravage, if they win the fight.

Such was the gory nurse that trained societies to cohesiveness. We inherit the warlike type; and for most of the capacities of heroism that the human race is full of we have to thank this cruel history. Dead men tell no tales, and if there were any tribes of other type than this they have left no survivors. Our ancestors have bred pugnacity into our bone and marrow, and thousands of years of peace won't breed it out of us. The popular imagination fairly fattens on the thought of wars. Let public opinion once reach a certain fighting pitch, and no ruler can withstand it. In the Boer war both governments began with bluff but could n't stay there, the military tension was too much for them. In 1898 our people had read the word "war" in letters three inches high for three months in every newspaper. The pliant politician McKinley was swept away by their eagerness, and our squalid war with Spain became a necessity.

At the present day, civilized opinion is a

curious mental mixture. The military instincts and ideals are as strong as ever, but are confronted by reflective criticisms which sorely curb their ancient freedom. Innumerable writers are showing up the bestial side of military service. Pure loot and mastery seem no longer morally avowable motives, and pretexts must be found for attributing them solely to the enemy. England and we, our army and navy authorities repeat without ceasing, arm solely for "peace," Germany and Japan it is who are bent on loot and glory. "Peace" in military mouths to-day is a synonym for "war expected." The word has become a pure provocative, and no government wishing peace sincerely should allow it ever to be printed in a newspaper. Every up-to-date dictionary should say that "peace" and "war" mean the same thing, now *in posse*, now *in actu*. It may even reasonably be said that the intensely sharp competitive *preparation* for war by the nations *is the real war*, permanent, unceasing; and that the battles are only a sort of public verification of the mastery gained during the "peace"-interval.

It is plain that on this subject civilized man has developed a sort of double personality. If we take European nations, no legitimate interest of any one of them would seem to justify the tremendous destructions which a war to compass it would necessarily entail. It would seem as though common sense and reason ought to find a way to reach agreement in every conflict of honest interests. I myself think it our bounden duty to believe in such international rationality as possible. But, as things stand, I see how desperately hard it is to bring the peace-party and the war-party together, and I believe that the difficulty is due to certain deficiencies in the program of pacificism which set the militarist imagination strongly, and to a certain extent justifiably, against it. In the whole discussion both sides are on imaginative and sentimental ground. It is but one utopia against another, and everything one says must be abstract and hypothetical. Subject to this criticism and caution, I will try to characterize in abstract strokes the opposite imaginative forces, and point out what to my own very fallible mind seems the best utopian hypothesis, the most promising line of conciliation.

In my remarks, pacificist though I am, I will refuse to speak of the bestial side of the war-*régime* (already done justice to by many writers) and consider only the higher aspects of militaristic sentiment. Patriotism no one thinks discreditable; nor does any one deny that war is the romance of history. But inordinate ambitions are the soul of every patriotism, and the possibility of violent death the soul of all romance. The militarily patriotic and romantic-minded everywhere, and especially the professional military class, refuse to admit for a moment that war may be. a transitory phenomenon in social evolution. The notion of a sheep's paradise like that revolts, they say, our higher imagination. Where then would be the steeps of life? If war had ever stopped, we should have to re-invent it, on this view, to redeem life from flat degeneration.

Reflective apologists for war at the present day all take it religiously. It is a sort of sacrament. Its profits are to the vanquished as well as to the victor; and quite apart from any question of profit, it is an absolute good, we are told, for it is human nature at its highest dynamic. Its "horrors" are a cheap price to pay for rescue from the only alternative supposed, of a world of clerks and teachers, of co-education and zo-ophily, of "consumer's leagues" and "associated charities," of industrialism unlimited, and femininism unabashed. No scorn, no hardness, no valor any more! Fie upon such a cattleyard of a planet!

So fas as the central essence of this feeling goes, no healthy minded person, it seems to me, can help to some degree partaking of it. Militarism is the great preserver of our ideals of hardihood, and human life with no use for hardihood would be contemptible. Without risks or prizes for the darer, history would be insipid indeed; and there is a type of military character which every one feels that the race should never cease to breed, for every one is sensitive to its superiority. The duty is incumbent on mankind, of keeping military characters in stock — of keeping them, if not for use, then as ends in themselves and as pure pieces of perfection, — so that Roosevelt's weaklings and molly-coddles may not end by making everything else disappear from the face of nature.

This natural sort of feeling forms, I think, the innermost soul of army-writings. Without any exception known to me, militarist authors take a highly mystical view of their subject, and regard war as a biological or sociological necessity, uncontrolled by ordinary psychological checks and motives. When the time of development is ripe the war must come, reason or no reason, for the justifications pleaded are invariably fictitious. War is, in short, a permanent human *obligation*. General Homer Lea, in his recent book "The Valor of Ignorance," plants himself squarely on this ground. Readiness for war is for him the essence of nationality, and ability in it the supreme measure of the health of nations.

Nations, General Lea says, are never stationary — they must necessarily expand or shrink, according to their vitality or decrepitude. Japan now is culminating; and by the fatal law in question it is impossible that her statesmen should not long since have entered, with extraordinary foresight, upon a vast policy of conquest — the game in which the first moves were her wars with China and Russia and her treaty with England, and of which the final objective is the capture of the Philippines, the Hawaiian Islands, Alaska, and the whole of our Coast west of the Sierra Passes. This will give Japan what her ineluctable vocation as a state absolutely forces her to claim, the possession of the entire Pacific Ocean; and to oppose these deep designs we Americans have, according to our author, nothing but our conceit, our ignorance, our commercialism, our corruption, and our feminism. General Lea makes a minute technical

comparison of the military strength which we
at present could oppose to the strength of
Japan, and concludes that the islands, Alaska,
Oregon, and Southern California, would fall
almost without resistance, that San Francisco
must surrender in a fortnight to a Japanese investment, that in three or four months the
war would be over, and our republic, unable to
regain what it had heedlessly neglected to
protect sufficiently, would then "disintegrate,"
until perhaps some Cæsar should arise to weld
us again into a nation.

A dismal forecast indeed! Yet not unplausible, if the mentality of Japan's statesmen be of the Cæsarian type of which history
shows so many examples, and which is all that
General Lea seems able to imagine. But
there is no reason to think that women can
no longer be the mothers of Napoleonic or
Alexandrian characters; and if these come in
Japan and find their opportunity, just such
surprises as "The Valor of Ignorance" paints
may lurk in ambush for us. Ignorant as we
still are of the innermost recesses of Japanese

mentality, we may be foolhardy to disregard such possibilities.

Other militarists are more complex and more moral in their considerations. The "Philosophie des Krieges," by S. R. Steinmetz is a good example. War, according to this author, is an ordeal instituted by God, who weighs the nations in its balance. It is the essential form of the State, and the only function in which peoples can employ all their powers at once and convergently. No victory is possible save as the resultant of a totality of virtues, no defeat for which some vice or weakness is not responsible. · Fidelity, cohesiveness, tenacity, heroism, conscience, education, inventiveness, economy, wealth, physical health and vigor — there is n't a moral or intellectual point of superiority that does n't tell, when God holds his assizes and hurls the peoples upon one another. *Die Weltgeschichte ist das Weltgericht;* and Dr. Steinmetz does not believe that in the long run chance and luck play any part in apportioning the issues.

The virtues that prevail, it must be noted,

are virtues anyhow, superiorities that count in peaceful as well as in military competition; but the strain on them, being infinitely intenser in the latter case, makes war infinitely more searching as a trial. No ordeal is comparable to its winnowings. Its dread hammer is the welder of men into cohesive states, and nowhere but in such states can human nature adequately develop its capacity. The only alternative is "degeneration."

Dr. Steinmetz is a conscientious thinker, and his book, short as it is, takes much into account. Its upshot can, it seems to me, be summed up in Simon Patten's word, that mankind was nursed in pain and fear, and that the transition to a "pleasure-economy" may be fatal to a being wielding no powers of defence against its disintegrative influences. If we speak of the *fear of emancipation from the fear-régime*, we put the whole situation into a single phrase; fear regarding ourselves now taking the place of the ancient fear of the enemy.

Turn the fear over as I will in my mind, it

all seems to lead back to two unwillingnesses of the imagination, one æsthetic, and the other moral; unwillingness, first to envisage a future in which army-life, with its many elements of charm, shall be forever impossible, and in which the destinies of peoples shall nevermore be decided quickly, thrillingly, and tragically, by force, but only gradually and insipidly by "evolution"; and, secondly, unwillingness to see the supreme theatre of human strenuousness closed, and the splendid military aptitudes of men doomed to keep always in a state of latency and never show themselves in action. These insistent unwillingnesses, no less than other æsthetic and ethical insistencies, have, it seems to me, to be listened to and respected. One cannot meet them effectively by mere counter-insistency on war's expensiveness and horror. The horror makes the thrill; and when the question is of getting the extremest and supremest out of human nature, talk of expense sounds ignominious. The weakness of so much merely negative criticism is evident — pacificism makes no converts from the military party. The military party denies neither the bestiality nor the horror, nor the expense; it only says that these things tell but half the story. It only says that war is *worth* them; that, taking human nature as a whole, its wars are its best protection against its weaker and more cowardly self, and that mankind cannot *afford* to adopt a peace-economy.

Pacificists ought to enter more deeply into the æsthetical and ethical point of view of their opponents. Do that first in any controversy, says J. J. Chapman, *then move the point,* and your opponent will follow. So long as anti-militarists propose no substitute for war's disciplinary function, no *moral equivalent* of war, analogous, as one might say, to the mechanical equivalent of heat, so long they fail to realize the full inwardness of the situation. And as a rule they do fail. The duties, penalties, and sanctions pictured in the utopias they paint are all too weak and tame to touch the military-minded. Tolstoi's pacificism is the only exception to this rule, for it is profoundly pessimistic as regards all this world's values, and makes the fear of the Lord furnish the moral spur provided elsewhere by the fear of the enemy. But our socialistic peace-advocates all believe absolutely in this world's values; and instead of the fear of the Lord and the fear of the enemy, the only fear they reckon with is the fear of poverty if one be lazy. This weakness pervades all the socialistic literature with which I am acquainted. Even in Lowes Dickinson's exquisite dialogue,[1] high wages and short hours are the only forces invoked for overcoming man's distaste for repulsive kinds of labor. Meanwhile men at large still live as they always have lived, under a pain-and-fear economy — for those of us who live in an ease-economy are but an island in the stormy ocean — and the whole atmosphere of present-day utopian literature tastes mawkish and dishwatery to people who still keep a sense for life's more bitter flavors. It suggests, in truth, ubiquitous inferiority.

Inferiority is always with us, and merciless

[1] "Justice and Liberty," N. Y., 1909.

scorn of it is the keynote of the military temper. "Dogs, would you live forever?" shouted Frederick the Great. "Yes," say our utopians, "let us live forever, and raise our level gradually." The best thing about our "inferiors" to-day is that they are as tough as nails, and physically and morally almost as insensitive. Utopianism would see them soft and squeamish, while militarism would keep their callousness, but transfigure it into a meritorious characteristic, needed by "the service," and redeemed by that from the suspicion of inferiority. All the qualities of a man acquire dignity when he knows that the service of the collectivity that owns him needs them. If proud of the collectivity, his own pride rises in proportion. No collectivity is like an army for nourishing such pride; but it has to be confessed that the only sentiment which the image of pacific cosmopolitan industrialism is capable of arousing in countless worthy breasts is shame at the idea of belonging to *such* a collectivity. It is obvious that the United States of America as they exist to-day impress a mind like General Lea's as so much human blubber. Where is the sharpness and precipitousness, the contempt for life, whether one's own, or another's? Where is the savage "yes" and "no," the unconditional duty? Where is the conscription? Where is the blood-tax? Where is anything that one feels honored by belonging to?

Having said thus much in preparation, I will now confess my own utopia. I devoutly believe in the reign of peace and in the gradual advent of some sort of a socialistic equilibrium. The fatalistic view of the war-function is to me nonsense, for I know that war-making is due to definite motives and subject to prudential checks and reasonable criticisms, just like any other form of enterprise. And when whole nations are the armies, and the science of destruction vies in intellectual refinement with the sciences of production, I see that war becomes absurd and impossible from its own monstrosity. Extravagant ambitions will have to be replaced by reasonable claims, and nations must make common cause against them. I see no reason why all this should not apply to yellow as well as to white countries, and I look forward to a future when acts of war shall be formally outlawed as between civilized peoples.

All these beliefs of mine put me squarely into the anti-militarist party. But I do not believe that peace either ought to be or will be permanent on this globe, unless the states pacifically organized preserve some of the old elements of army-discipline. A permanently successful peace-economy cannot be a simple pleasure-economy. In the more or less socialistic future towards which mankind seems drifting we must still subject ourselves collectively to those severities which answer to our real position upon this only partly hospitable globe. We must make new energies and hardihoods continue the manliness to which the military mind so faithfully clings. Martial virtues must be the enduring cement; intrepidity, contempt of softness, surrender of private interest, obedience to command, must still remain the rock upon which states are built — unless, indeed, we wish for dangerous reactions against commonwealths fit only for contempt, and liable to invite attack whenever a centre of crystallization for military-minded enterprise gets formed anywhere in their neighborhood.

The war-party is assuredly right in affirming and reaffirming that the martial virtues, although originally gained by the race through war, are absolute and permanent human goods. Patriotic pride and ambition in their military form are, after all, only specifications of a more general competitive passion. They are its first form, but that is no reason for supposing them to be its last form. Men now are proud of belonging to a conquering nation, and without a murmur they lay down their persons and their wealth, if by so doing they may fend off subjection. But who can be sure that *other aspects of one's country* may not, with time and education and suggestion enough, come to be regarded with similarly effective feelings of pride and shame? Why should men not some day feel that it is worth a blood-tax to belong to a collectivity superior in *any* ideal respect? Why should they not blush with indignant shame if the community that owns them is vile in any way whatsoever? Individuals, daily more numerous, now feel this civic passion. It is only a question of blowing on the spark till the whole population gets incandescent, and on the ruins of the old morals of military honor, a stable system of morals of civic honor builds itself up. What the whole community comes to believe in grasps the individual as in a vise. The war-function has grasped us so far; but constructive interests may some day seem no less imperative, and impose on the individual a hardly lighter burden.

Let me illustrate my idea more concretely. There is nothing to make one indignant in the mere fact that life is hard, that men should toil and suffer pain. The planetary conditions once for all are such, and we can stand it.

But that so many men, by mere accidents of birth and opportunity, should have a life of *nothing else* but toil and pain and hardness and inferiority imposed upon them, should have *no* vacation, while others natively no more deserving never get any taste of this campaigning life at all, — *this* is capable of arousing indignation in reflective minds. It may end by seeming shameful to all of us that some of us have nothing but campaigning, and others nothing but unmanly ease. If now — and this is my idea — there were, instead of military conscription a conscription of the whole youthful population to form for a certain number of years a part of the army enlisted against *Nature*, the injustice would tend to be evened out, and numerous other goods to the commonwealth would follow. The military ideals of hardihood and discipline would be wrought into the growing fibre of the people; no one would remain blind as the luxurious classes now are blind, to man's relations to the globe he lives on, and to the permanently sour and hard foundations of his higher life. To coal and iron mines, to freight trains, to fishing fleets in December, to dishwashing, clothes-washing, and window-washing, to road-building and tunnel-making, to foundries and stoke-holes, and to the frames of skyscrapers, would our gilded youths be drafted off, according to their choice, to get the childishness knocked out of them, and to come back into society with healthier sympathies and soberer ideas. They would have paid their blood-tax, done their own part in the immemorial human warfare against nature; they would tread the earth more proudly, the women would value them more highly, they would be better fathers and teachers of the following generation.

Such a conscription, with the state of public opinion that would have required it, and the many moral fruits it would bear, would preserve in the midst of a pacific civilization the manly virtues which the military party is so afraid of seeing disappear in peace. We should get toughness without callousness, authority with as little criminal cruelty as possible, and painful work done cheerily because the duty is temporary, and threatens not, as now, to degrade the whole remainder of one's life. I spoke of the "moral equivalent" of war. So far, war has been the only force that can discipline a whole community, and until an equivalent discipline is organized, I believe that war must have its way. But I have no serious doubt that the ordinary prides and shames of social man, once developed to a certain intensity, are capable of organizing such a moral equivalent as I have sketched, or some other just as effective for preserving manliness of type. It is but a question of time, of skilful propagandism, and of opinion-making men seizing historic opportunities.

The martial type of character can be bred without war. Strenuous honor and disinterestedness abound elsewhere. Priests and medical men are in a fashion educated to it, and we should all feel some degree of it imperative if we were conscious of our work as an obligatory service to the state. We should be *owned*, as soldiers are by the army, and our pride would rise accordingly. We could be poor, then, without humiliation, as army officers now are. The only thing needed henceforward is to inflame the civic temper as past history has inflamed the military temper. H. G. Wells, as usual, sees the centre of the situation. "In many ways," he says, "military organization is the most peaceful of activities. When the contemporary man steps from the street, of clamorous insincere advertisement, push, adulteration, underselling and intermittent employment into the barrack-yard, he steps on to a higher social plane, into an atmosphere of service and cooperation and of infinitely more honorable emulations. Here at least men are not flung out of employment to degenerate because there is no immediate work for them to do. They are fed and drilled and trained for better services. Here at least a man is supposed to win promotion by self-forgetfulness and not by self-seeking. And beside

the feeble and irregular endowment of research by commercialism, its little short-
sighted snatches at profit by innovation and
scientific economy, see how remarkable is the
steady and rapid development of method and
appliances in naval and military affairs!
Nothing is more striking than to compare the
progress of civil conveniences which has been
left almost entirely to the trader,ito the progress in military apparatus during the last
few decades. The house-appliances of to-day
for example, are little better than they were
fifty years ago. A house of to-day is still
almost as ill-ventilated, badly heated by
wasteful fires, clumsily arranged and furnished as the house of 1858. Houses a couple
of hundred years old are still satisfactory
places of residence, so little have our standards risen. But the rifle or battleship of
fifty years ago was beyond all comparison
inferior to those we possess; in power, in
speed, in convenience alike. No one has a
use now for such superannuated things."[1]

[1] " First and Last Things," 1908, p. 215.

Wells adds[1] that he thinks that the conceptions of order and discipline, the tradition of service and devotion, of physical fitness, unstinted exertion, and universal responsibility, which universal military duty is now teaching European nations, will remain a permanent acquisition, when the last ammunition has been used in the fireworks that celebrate the final peace. I believe as he does. It would be simply preposterous if the only force that could work ideals of honor and standards of efficiency into English or American natures should be the fear of being killed by the Germans or the Japanese. Great indeed is Fear; but it is not, as our military enthusiasts believe and try to make us believe, the only stimulus known for awakening the higher ranges of men's spiritual energy. The amount of alteration in public opinion which my utopia postulates is vastly less than the difference between the mentality of those black warriors who pursued Stanley's party on the Congo with their

[1] " First and Last Things," 1908, p, 226.

cannibal war-cry of "Meat! Meat!" and that of the "general-staff" of any civilized nation. History has seen the latter interval bridged over: the former one can be bridged over much more easily.

XII

REMARKS AT THE PEACE BANQUET

XII

REMARKS AT THE PEACE BANQUET [1]

I AM only a philosopher, and there is only one thing that a philosopher can be relied on to do, and that is, to contradict other philosophers. In ancient times philosophers defined man as the rational animal; and philosophers since then have always found much more to say about the rational than about the animal part of the definition. But looked at candidly, reason bears about the same proportion to the rest of human nature that we in this hall bear to the rest of America, Europe, Asia, Africa and Polynesia. Reason is one of the very feeblest of nature's forces, if you take it at only one spot and moment. It is only in the very long run that its effects become perceptible. Reason assumes to settle things by weighing them against each other

[1] Published in the Official Report of the Universal Peace Congress, held in Boston in 1904, and in the *Atlantic Monthly*, December, 1904.

without prejudice, partiality or excitement; but what affairs in the concrete are settled by is, and always will be, just prejudices, partialities, cupidities and excitements. Appealing to reason as we do, we are in a sort of forlorn-hope situation, like a small sand-bank in the midst of a hungry sea ready to wash it out of existence. But sand-banks grow when the conditions favor; and weak as reason is, it has this unique advantage over its antagonists that its activity never lets up and that it presses always in one direction, while men's prejudices vary, their passions ebb and flow, and their excitements are intermittent. Our sand-bank, I absolutely believe, is bound to grow. Bit by bit it will get dyked and breakwatered. But sitting as we do in this warm room, with music and lights and smiling faces, it is easy to get too sanguine about our task; and since I am called to speak, I feel as if it might not be out of place to say a word about the strength of our enemy.

Our permanent enemy is the rooted bellicosity of human nature. Man, biologically considered, and whatever else he may be into the bargain, is the most formidable of all beasts of prey, and, indeed, the only one that preys systematically on his own species. We are once for all adapted to the military status. A millennium of peace would not breed the fighting disposition out of our bone and marrow, and a function so ingrained and vital will never consent to die without resistance, and will always find impassioned apologists and idealizers.

Not only men born to be soldiers, but noncombatants by trade and nature, historians in their studies, and clergymen in their pulpits, have been war's idealizers. They have talked of war as of God's court of justice. And, indeed, if we think how many things beside the frontiers of states the wars of history have decided, we must feel some respectful awe, in spite of all the horrors. Our actual civilization, good and bad alike, has had past wars for its determining condition. Great mindedness among the tribes of men has always meant the will to prevail, and all the more so if prevailing included slaughtering and being slaughtered. Rome, Paris, England, Brandenburg, Piedmont, — possibly soon Japan, — along with their arms have their traits of character and habits of thought prevail among their conquered neighbors. The blessings we actually enjoy, such as they are, have grown up in the shadow of the wars of antiquity. The various ideals were backed by fighting wills, and when neither would give way, the God of battles had to be the arbiter. A shallow view this, truly; for who can say what might have prevailed if man had ever been a reasoning and not a fighting animal? Like dead men, dead causes tell no tales, and the ideals that went under in the past, along with all the tribes that represented them, find to-day no recorder, no explainer, no defender.

But apart from theoretic defenders, and apart from every soldierly individual straining at the leash and clamoring for opportunity, war has an omnipotent support in the form of our imagination. Man lives *by* habits indeed, but what he lives *for* is thrills and excitements. The only relief from habit's tediousness is periodical excitement. From time immemorial wars have been, especially for non-combatants, the supremely thrilling excitement. Heavy and dragging at its end, at its outset every war means an explosion of imaginative energy. The dams of routine burst, and boundless prospects open. The remotest spectators share the fascination of that awful struggle now in process on the confines of the world. There is not a man in this room, I suppose, who doesn't buy both an evening and a morning paper, and first of all pounce on the war column.

A deadly listlessness would come over most men's imagination of the future if they could seriously be brought to believe that never again *in sæcula sæculorum* would a war trouble human history. In such a stagnant summer afternoon of a world, where would be the zest or interest?

This is the constitution of human nature

which we have to work against. The plain truth is that people *want* war. They want it anyhow; for itself, and apart from each and every possible consequence. It is the final bouquet of life's fireworks. The born soldiers want it hot and actual. The non-combatants want it in the background, and always as an open possibility, to feed imagination on and keep excitement going. Its clerical and historical defenders fool themselves when they talk as they do about it. What moves them is not the blessings it has won for us, but a vague religious exaltation. War is human nature at its uttermost. We are here to do our uttermost. It is a sacrament. Society would rot without the mystical blood-payment.

We do ill, I think, therefore, to talk much of universal peace or of a general disarmament. We must go in for preventive medicine, not for radical cure. We must cheat our foe, circumvent him in detail, not try to change his nature. In one respect war is like love, though in no other. Both leave us intervals of rest; and in the intervals life goes on perfectly well without them, though the imagination still dallies with their possibility. Equally insane when once aroused and under headway, whether they shall be aroused or not depends on accidental circumstances. How are old maids and old bachelors made? Not by deliberate vows of celibacy, but by sliding on from year to year with no sufficient matrimonial provocation. So of the nations with their wars. Let the general possibility of war be left open, in Heaven's name, for the imagination to dally with. Let the soldiers dream of killing, as the old maids dream of marrying.

But organize in every conceivable way the practical machinery for making each successive chance of war abortive. Put peace men in power; educate the editors and statesmen to responsibility. How beautifully did their trained responsibility in England make the Venezuela incident abortive! Seize every pretext, however small, for arbitration methods, and multiply the precedents; foster

305

rival excitements, and invent new outlets for heroic energy; and from one generation to another the chances are that irritation will grow less acute and states of strain less dangerous among the nations. Armies and navies will continue, of course, and fire the minds of populations with their potentialities of greatness. But their officers will find that somehow or other, with no deliberate intention on any one's part, each successive "incident" has managed to evaporate and to lead nowhere, and that the thought of what might have been remains their only consolation.

The last weak runnings of the war spirit will be "punitive expeditions." A country that turns its arms only against uncivilized foes is, I think, wrongly taunted as degenerate. Of course it has ceased to be heroic in the old grand style. But I verily believe that this is because it now sees something better. It has a conscience. It will still perpetrate peccadillos. But it is afraid, afraid in the good sense, to engage in absolute crimes against civilization.

XIII

THE SOCIAL VALUE OF THE COLLEGE-BRED

XIII

THE SOCIAL VALUE OF THE COLLEGE-BRED[1]

Of what use is a college training? We who have had it seldom hear the question raised; we might be a little nonplussed to answer it offhand. A certain amount of meditation has brought me to this as the pithiest reply which I myself can give: The best claim that a college education can possibly make on your respect, the best thing it can aspire to accomplish for you, is this: that it should *help you to know a good man when you see him*. This is as true of women's as of men's colleges; but that it is neither a joke nor a one-sided abstraction I shall now endeavor to show.

What talk do we commonly hear about the contrast between college education and the education which business or technical or pro-

---

[1] Address delivered at a meeting of the Association of American Alumnæ at Radcliffe College, November 7, 1907, and first published in *McClure's Magazine* for February, 1908.

fessional schools confer? The college education is called higher because it is supposed to
be so general and so disinterested. At the
"schools" you get a relatively narrow practical skill, you are told, whereas the "colleges" give you the more liberal culture, the
broader outlook, the historical perspective, the
philosophic atmosphere, or something which
phrases of that sort try to express. You are
made into an efficient instrument for doing a
definite thing, you hear, at the schools; but,
apart from that, you may remain a crude and
smoky kind of petroleum, incapable of spreading light. The universities and colleges, on
the other hand, although they may leave you
less efficient for this or that practical task,
suffuse your whole mentality with something
more important than skill. They redeem you,
make you well-bred; they make "good company" of you mentally. If they find you with
a naturally boorish or caddish mind, they
cannot leave you so, as a technical school
may leave you. This, at least, is pretended;
this is what we hear among college-trained

people when they compare their education with every other sort. Now, exactly how much does this signify?

It is certain, to begin with, that the narrowest trade or professional training does something more for a man than to make a skilful practical tool of him — it makes him also a judge of other men's skill. Whether his trade be pleading at the bar or surgery or plastering or plumbing, it develops a critical sense in him for that sort of occupation. He understands the difference between second-rate and first-rate work in his whole branch of industry; he gets to know a good job in his own line as soon as he sees it; and getting to know this in his own line, he gets a faint sense of what good work may mean anyhow, that may, if circumstances favor, spread into his judgments elsewhere. Sound work, clean work, finished work: feeble work, slack work, sham work — these words express an identical contrast in many different departments of activity. In so far forth, then, even the humblest manual trade may beget in one a certain small degree of power to judge of good work generally.

Now, what is supposed to be the line of us who have the higher college training? Is there any broader line — since our education claims primarily not to be "narrow" — in which we also are made good judges between what is first-rate and what is second-rate only? What is especially taught in the colleges has long been known by the name of the "humanities," and these are often identified with Greek and Latin. But it is only as literatures, not as languages, that Greek and Latin have any general humanity-value; so that in a broad sense the humanities mean literature primarily, and in a still broader sense the study of masterpieces in almost any field of human endeavor. Literature keeps the primacy; for it not only *consists* of masterpieces, but is largely *about* masterpieces, being little more than an appreciative chronicle of human master-strokes, so far as it takes the form of criticism and history. You can give humanistic value to almost anything by teaching it historically. Geology, economics, mechanics, are humanities when taught with reference to the successive achievements of the geniuses to which these sciences owe their being. Not taught thus literature remains grammar, art a catalogue, history a list of dates, and natural science a sheet of formulas and weights and measures.

The sifting of human creations! — nothing less than this is what we ought to mean by the humanities. Essentially this means biography; what our colleges should teach is, therefore, biographical history, that not of politics merely, but of anything and everything so far as human efforts and conquests are factors that have played their part. Studying in this way, we learn what types of activity have stood the test of time; we acquire standards of the excellent and durable. All our arts and sciences and institutions are but so many quests of perfection on the part of men; and when we see how diverse the types of excellence may be, how various the tests, how flexible the adaptations, we gain a richer sense of what the terms "better" and "worse" may signify in general. Our critical sensibilities grow both more acute and less fanatical. We sympathize with men's mistakes even in the act of penetrating them; we feel the pathos of lost causes and misguided epochs even while we applaud what overcame them.

Such words are vague and such ideas are inadequate, but their meaning is unmistakable. What the colleges — teaching humanities by examples which may be special, but which must be typical and pregnant — should at least try to give us, is a general sense of what, under various disguises, *superiority* has always signified and may still signify. The feeling for a good human job anywhere, the admiration of the really admirable, the disesteem of what is cheap and trashy and impermanent, — this is what we call the critical sense, the sense for ideal values. It is the better part of what men know as wisdom. Some of us are wise in this way naturally and by genius; some of us never become so. But to have spent one's youth at college, in contact with the choice and rare and precious, and yet still to be a blind prig or vulgarian, unable to scent out human excellence or to divine it amid its accidents, to know it only when ticketed and labelled and forced on us by others, this indeed should be accounted the very calamity and shipwreck of a higher education.

The sense for human superiority ought, then, to be considered our line, as boring subways is the engineer's line and the surgeon's is appendicitis. Our colleges ought to have lit up in us a lasting relish for the better kind of man, a loss of appetite for mediocrities, and a disgust for cheapjacks. We ought to smell, as it were, the difference of quality in men and their proposals when we enter the world of affairs about us. Expertness in this might well atone for some of our awkwardness at accounts, for some of our ignorance of dynamos. The best claim we can make for the higher education, the best single phrase in which we can tell what it ought to do for us, is, then, exactly what I said: it should enable us to *know a good man when we see him.*

That the phrase is anything but an empty epigram follows from the fact that if you ask in what line it is most important that a democracy like ours should have its sons and daughters skilful, you see that it is this line more than any other. "The people in their wisdom" — this is the kind of wisdom most needed by the people. Democracy is on its trial, and no one knows how it will stand the ordeal. Abounding about us are pessimistic prophets. Fickleness and violence used to be, but are no longer, the vices which they charge to democracy. What its critics now affirm is that its preferences are inveterately for the inferior. So it was in the beginning, they say, and so it will be world without end. Vulgarity enthroned and institutionalized, elbowing everything superior from the highway, this, they tell us, is our irremediable destiny; and the picture-papers of the European continent are already drawing Uncle Sam with the hog instead of the eagle for his heraldic emblem. The privileged aristocracies of the foretime, with all their iniquities, did at least preserve some taste for higher human quality, and honor certain forms of refinement by their enduring traditions. But when democracy is sovereign, its doubters say, nobility will form a sort of invisible church, and sincerity and refinement, stripped of honor, precedence, and favor, will have to vegetate on sufferance in private corners. They will have no general influence. They will be harmless eccentricities.

Now, who can be absolutely certain that this may not be the career of democracy? Nothing future is quite secure; states enough have inwardly rotted; and democracy as a whole may undergo self-poisoning. But, on the other hand, democracy is a kind of religion, and we are bound not to admit its failure. Faiths and utopias are the noblest exercise of human reason, and no one with a spark of reason in him will sit down fatalistically before the croaker's picture. The best of us are filled with the contrary vision of a democracy stumbling through every error till its institutions glow with justice and its customs shine with beauty. Our better men *shall* show the way and we *shall* follow them; so we are brought round again to the mission of the higher education in helping us to know the better kind of man whenever we see him.

The notion that a people can run itself and its affairs anonymously is now well known to be the silliest of absurdities. Mankind does nothing save through initiatives on the part of inventors, great or small, and imitation by the rest of us — these are the sole factors active in human progress. Individuals of genius show the way, and set the patterns, which common people then adopt and follow. *The rivalry of the patterns is the history of the world.* Our democratic problem thus is statable in ultra-simple terms: Who are the kind of men from whom our majorities shall take their cue? Whom shall they treat as rightful leaders? We and our leaders are the x and the y of the equation here; all other historic circumstances, be they economical, political, or intellectual, are only the background of occasion on which the living drama works itself out between us.

In this very simple way does the value of our educated class define itself: we more than others should be able to divine the worthier and better leaders. The terms here are monstrously simplified, of course, but such a bird's-eye view lets us immediately take our bearings. In our democracy, where everything else is so shifting, we alumni and alumnæ of the colleges are the only permanent presence that corresponds to the aristocracy in older countries. We have continuous traditions, as they have; our motto, too, is *noblesse oblige;* and, unlike them, we stand for ideal interests solely, for we have no corporate selfishness and wield no powers of corruption. We ought to have our own class-consciousness. *"Les Intellectuels!"* What prouder club-name could there be than this one, used ironically by the party of "redblood," the party of every stupid prejudice and passion, during the anti-Dreyfus craze, to satirize the men in France who still retained some critical sense and judgment! Critical sense, it has to be confessed, is not an exciting term, hardly a banner to carry in processions. Affections for old habit, currents of self-interest, and gales of passion are the forces that keep the human ship moving; and the pressure of the judicious pilot's hand upon the tiller is a relatively insignificant energy. But the affections, passions, and interests are shifting, successive, and distraught; they blow in alternation while the pilot's hand is steadfast. He knows the compass, and, with all the lee-ways he is obliged to tack toward, he always makes some headway. A small force, if it never lets up, will accumulate effects more considerable than those of much greater forces if these work inconsistently. The ceaseless whisper of the more permanent ideals, the steady tug of truth and justice, give them but time, *must* warp the world in their direction.

This bird's-eye view of the general steering function of the college-bred amid the driftings of democracy ought to help us to a wider vision of what our colleges themselves should aim at. If we are to be the yeast-cake for democracy's dough, if we are to make it rise with culture's preferences, we must see to it that culture spreads broad sails. We must shake the old double reefs out of the canvas into the wind and sunshine, and let in every modern subject, sure that any subject will prove humanistic, if its setting be kept only wide enough.

Stevenson says somewhere to his reader: "You think you are just making this bargain, but you are really laying down a link in the policy of mankind." Well, your technical school should enable you to make your bargain splendidly; but your college should show you just the place of that kind of bargain — a pretty poor place, possibly — in the whole policy of mankind. That is the kind of liberal outlook, of perspective, of atmosphere, which should surround every subject as a college deals with it.

We of the colleges must eradicate a curious notion which numbers of good people have about such ancient seats of learning as Harvard. To many ignorant outsiders, that name suggests little more than a kind of sterilized conceit and incapacity for being pleased. In Edith Wyatt's exquisite book of Chicago sketches called "Every One his Own Way" there is a couple who stand for culture in the sense of exclusiveness, Richard Elliot and his feminine counterpart — feeble caricatures of mankind, unable to know any good thing when they see it, incapable of enjoyment unless a printed label gives them leave. Possibly this type of culture may exist near Cambridge and Boston. There may be specimens there, for priggishness is just like painter's colic or any other trade-disease. But every good college makes its students immune against this malady, of which the microbe haunts the neighborhood of printed pages. It does so by its general tone being too hearty for the microbe's life. Real culture lives by sympathies and admirations, not by dislikes and disdains; under all misleading wrappings it pounces unerringly upon the human core.

If a college, through the inferior human influences that have grown regnant there, fails to catch the robuster tone, its failure is colossal, for its social function stops: democracy gives it a wide berth, turns toward it a deaf ear.

"Tone," to be sure, is a terribly vague word to use, but there is no other, and this whole meditation is over questions of tone. By their tone are all things human either lost or saved. If democracy is to be saved it must catch the higher, healthier tone. If we are to impress it with our preferences, we ourselves must use the proper tone, which we, in turn, must have caught from our own teachers. It all reverts in the end to the action of innumerable imitative individuals upon each other and to the question of whose tone has the highest spreading power. As a class, we college graduates should look to it that *ours* has spreading power. It ought to have the highest spreading power.

In our essential function of indicating the better men, we now have formidable competitors outside. *McClure's Magazine*, the

American Magazine, *Collier's Weekly*, and, in its fashion, the *World's Work*, constitute together a real popular university along this very line. It would be a pity if any future historian were to have to write words like these: "By the middle of the twentieth century the higher institutions of learning had lost all influence over public opinion in the United States. But the mission of raising the tone of democracy, which they had proved themselves so lamentably unfitted to exert, was assumed with rare enthusiasm and prosecuted with extraordinary skill and success by a new educational power; and for the clarification of their human sympathies and elevation of their human preferences, the people at large acquired the habit of resorting exclusively to the guidance of certain private literary adventures, commonly designated in the market by the affectionate name of ten-cent magazines."

Must not we of the colleges see to it that no historian shall ever say anything like this? Vague as the phrase of knowing a good man

when you see him may be, diffuse and indefinite as one must leave its application, is there
any other formula that describes so well the
result at which our institutions *ought* to aim?
If they do that, they do the best thing conceivable. If they fail to do it, they fail in very
deed. It surely is a fine synthetic formula.
If our faculties and graduates could once
collectively come to realize it as the great
underlying purpose toward which they have
always been more or less obscurely groping,
a great clearness would be shed over many of
their problems; and, as for their influence
in the midst of our social system, it would
embark upon a new career of strength.

XIV

THE UNIVERSITY AND
THE INDIVIDUAL

I. THE PH.D. OCTOPUS[1]

SOME years ago we had at our Harvard
Graduate School a very brilliant student of
Philosophy, who, after leaving us and sup-
porting himself by literary labor for three
years, received an appointment to teach
English Literature at a sister-institution of
learning. The governors of this institution,
however, had no sooner communicated the
appointment than they made the awful
discovery that they had enrolled upon their
staff a person who was unprovided with the
Ph.D. degree. The man in question had
been satisfied to work at Philosophy for her
own sweet (or bitter) sake, and had disdained
to consider that an academic bauble should
be his reward.

His appointment had thus been made under
a misunderstanding. He was not the proper
man; and there was nothing to do but to

[1] Published in the *Harvard Monthly*, March, 1903.

inform him of the fact. It was notified to him
by his new President that his appointment
must be revoked, or that a Harvard doctor's
degree must forthwith be procured.

Although it was already the spring of the
year, our Subject, being a man of spirit, took
up the challenge, turned his back upon literature (which in view of his approaching duties
might have seemed his more urgent concern)
and spent the weeks that were left him, in
writing a metaphysical thesis and grinding
his psychology, logic and history of philosophy up again, so as to pass our formidable
ordeals.

When the thesis came to be read by our
committee, we could not pass it. Brilliancy
and originality by themselves won't save a
thesis for the doctorate; it must also exhibit
a heavy technical apparatus of learning; and
this our candidate had neglected to bring to
bear. So, telling him that he was temporarily
rejected, we advised him to pad out the thesis
properly, and return with it next year, at the
same time informing his new President that

this signified nothing as to his merits, that he was of ultra Ph.D. quality, and one of the strongest men with whom we had ever had to deal.

To our surprise we were given to understand in reply that the quality *per se* of the man signified nothing in this connection, and that three magical letters were the thing seriously required. The College had always gloried in a list of faculty members who bore the doctor's title, and to make a gap in the galaxy, and admit a common fox without a tail, would be a degradation impossible to be thought of. We wrote again, pointing out that a Ph.D. in philosophy would prove little anyhow as to one's ability to teach literature; we sent separate letters in which we outdid each other in eulogy of our candidate's powers, for indeed they were great; and at last, *mirabile dictu*, our eloquence prevailed. He was allowed to retain his appointment provisionally, on condition that one year later at the farthest his miserably naked name should be prolonged by the sacred appendage the lack of which had given so much trouble to all concerned.

Accordingly he came up here the following spring with an adequate thesis (known since in print as a most brilliant contribution to metaphysics), passed a first-rate examination, wiped out the stain, and brought his college into proper relations with the world again. Whether his teaching, during that first year, of English Literature was made any the better by the impending examination in a different subject, is a question which I will not try to solve.

I have related this incident at such length because it is so characteristic of American academic conditions at the present day. Graduate schools still are something of a novelty, and higher diplomas something of a rarity. The latter, therefore, carry a vague sense of preciousness and honor, and have a particularly "up-to-date" appearance, and it is no wonder if smaller institutions, unable to attract professors already eminent, and forced usually to recruit their faculties from the relatively young, should hope to compensate for the obscurity of the names of their officers of instruction by the abundance of decorative titles by which those names are followed on the pages of the catalogues where they appear. The dazzled reader of the list, the parent or student, says to himself, "This must be a terribly distinguished crowd, — their titles shine like the stars in the firmament; Ph.D.'s, S.D.'s, and Litt.D.'s, bespangle the page as if they were sprinkled over it from a pepper caster."

Human nature is once for all so childish that every reality becomes a sham somewhere, and in the minds of Presidents and Trustees the Ph.D. degree is in point of fact already looked upon as a mere advertising resource, a manner of throwing dust in the Public's eyes. "No instructor who is not a Doctor" has become a maxim in the smaller institutions which represent demand; and in each of the larger ones which represent supply, the same belief in decorated scholarship expresses itself in two antagonistic passions, one for multiplying as much as possible the annual output of doctors, the other for raising the standard of difficulty in passing, so that the Ph.D. of the special institution shall carry a higher blaze of distinction than it does elsewhere. Thus we at Harvard are proud of the number of candidates whom we reject, and of the inability of men who are not *distingués* in intellect to pass our tests.

America is thus as a nation rapidly drifting towards a state of things in which no man of science or letters will be accounted respectable unless some kind of badge or diploma is stamped upon him, and in which bare personality will be a mark of outcast estate. It seems to me high time to rouse ourselves to consciousness, and to cast a critical eye upon this decidedly grotesque tendency. Other nations suffer terribly from the Mandarin disease. Are we doomed to suffer like the rest?

Our higher degrees were instituted for the laudable purpose of stimulating scholarship, especially in the form of "original research."

THE PH.D. OCTOPUS

Experience has proved that great as the love of truth may be among men, it can be made still greater by adventitious rewards. The winning of a diploma certifying mastery and marking a barrier successfully passed, acts as a challenge to the ambitious; and if the diploma will help to gain bread-winning positions also, its power as a stimulus to work is tremendously increased. So far, we are on innocent ground; it is well for a country to have research in abundance, and our graduate schools do but apply a normal psychological spur. But the institutionizing on a large scale of any natural combination of need and motive always tends to run into technicality and to develop a tyrannical Machine with unforeseen powers of exclusion and corruption. Observation of the workings of our Harvard system for twenty years past has brought some of these drawbacks home to my consciousness, and I should like to call the attention of my readers to this disadvantageous aspect of the picture, and to make a couple of remedial suggestions, if I may.

335

In the first place, it would seem that to stimulate study, and to increase the *gelehrtes Publikum*, the class of highly educated men in our country, is the only positive good, and consequently the sole direct end at which our graduate schools, with their diploma-giving powers, should aim. If other results have developed they should be deemed secondary incidents, and if not desirable in themselves, they should be carefully guarded against.

To interfere with the free development of talent, to obstruct the natural play of supply and demand in the teaching profession, to foster academic snobbery by the prestige of certain privileged institutions, to transfer accredited value from essential manhood to an outward badge, to blight hopes and promote invidious sentiments, to divert the attention of aspiring youth from direct dealings with truth to the passing of examinations, — such consequences, if they exist, ought surely to be regarded as drawbacks to the system, and an enlightened public consciousness ought to be keenly alive to the importance of reducing their amount. Candidates themselves do seem to be keenly conscious of some of these evils, but outside of their ranks or in the general public no such consciousness, so far as I can see, exists; or if it does exist, it fails to express itself aloud. Schools, Colleges, and Universities, appear enthusiastic over the entire system, just as it stands, and unanimously applaud all its developments.

I beg the reader to consider some of the secondary evils which I have enumerated. First of all, is not our growing tendency to appoint no instructors who are not also doctors an instance of pure sham? Will any one pretend for a moment that the doctor's degree is a guarantee that its possessor will be successful as a teacher? Notoriously his moral, social and personal characteristics may utterly disqualify him for success in the class-room; and of these characteristics his doctor's examination is unable to take any account whatever. Certain bare human beings will always be better candidates for a given place than all the doctor-applicants on hand; and to exclude the former by a rigid rule, and in the end to have to sift the latter by private inquiry into their personal peculiarities among those who know them, just as if they were not doctors at all, is to stultify one's own procedure. You may say that at least you guard against ignorance of the subject by considering only the candidates who are doctors; but how then about making doctors in one subject teach a different subject? This happened in the instance by which I introduced this article, and it happens daily and hourly in all our colleges? The truth is that the Doctor-Monopoly in teaching, which is becoming so rooted an American custom, can show no serious grounds whatsoever for itself in reason. As it actually prevails and grows in vogue among us, it is due to childish motives exclusively. In reality it is but a sham, a bauble, a dodge, whereby to decorate the catalogues of schools and colleges.

Next, let us turn from the general promotion of a spirit of academic snobbery to the particular damage done to individuals by the system.

There are plenty of individuals so well endowed by nature that they pass with ease all the ordeals with which life confronts them. Such persons are born for professional success. Examinations have no terrors for them, and interfere in no way with their spiritual or worldly interests. There are others, not so gifted who nevertheless rise to the challenge, get a stimulus from the difficulty, and become doctors, not without some baleful nervous wear and tear and retardation of their purely inner life, but on the whole successfully, and with advantage. These two classes form the natural Ph.D.'s for whom the degree is legitimately instituted. To be sure, the degree is of no consequence one way or the other for the first sort of man, for in him the personal worth obviously outshines the title. To the second set of persons, however, the doctor ordeal may contribute a touch of energy and solidity of scholarship which otherwise they might have lacked, and were our candidates all drawn from these classes, no oppression would result from the institution.

But there is a third class of persons who are genuinely, and in the most pathetic sense, the institution's victims. For this type of character the academic life may become, after a certain point, a virulent poison. Men without marked originality or native force, but fond of truth and especially of books and study, ambitious of reward and recognition, poor often, and needing a degree to get a teaching position, weak in the eyes of their examiners, — among these we find the veritable *chair à canon* of the wars of learning, the unfit in the academic struggle for existence. There are individuals of this sort for whom to pass one degree after another seems the limit of earthly aspiration. Your private advice does not discourage them. They will fail, and go away to recuperate, and then present themselves for another ordeal, and sometimes prolong the process into middle life. Or else, if they are less heroic morally they

340

will accept the failure as a sentence of doom that they are not fit, and are broken-spirited men thereafter.

We of the university faculties are responsible for deliberately creating this new class of American social failures, and heavy is the responsibility. We advertise our "schools" and send out our degree-requirements, knowing well that aspirants of all sorts will be attracted, and at the same time we set a standard which intends to pass no man who has not native intellectual distinction. We know that there is no test, however absurd, by which, if a title or decoration, a public badge or mark, were to be won by it, some weakly suggestible or hauntable persons would not feel challenged, and remain unhappy if they went without it. We dangle our three magic letters before the eyes of these predestined victims, and they swarm to us like moths to an electric light. They come at a time when failure can no longer be repaired easily and when the wounds it leaves are permanent; and we say deliberately that mere work faithfully performed, as they perform it, will not by itself save them, they must in addition put in evidence the one thing they have not got, namely this quality of intellectual distinction. Occasionally, out of sheer human pity, we ignore our high and mighty standard and pass them. Usually, however, the standard, and not the candidate, commands our fidelity. The result is caprice, majorities of one on the jury, and on the whole a confession that our pretensions about the degree cannot be lived up to consistently. Thus, partiality in the favored cases; in the unfavored, blood on our hands; and in both a bad conscience, — are the results of our administration.

The more widespread becomes the popular belief that our diplomas are indispensable hall-marks to show the sterling metal of their holders, the more widespread these corruptions will become. We ought to look to the future carefully, for it takes generations for a national custom, once rooted, to be grown away from. All the European countries are seeking to diminish the check upon individual spontaneity which state examinations with their tyrannous growth have brought in their train. We have had to institute state examinations too; and it will perhaps be fortunate if some day hereafter our descendants, comparing machine with machine, do not sigh with regret for old times and American freedom, and wish that the *régime* of the dear old bosses might be reinstalled, with plain human nature, the glad hand and the marble heart, liking and disliking, and man-to-man relations grown possible again. Meanwhile, whatever evolution our state-examinations are destined to undergo, our universities at least should never cease to regard themselves as the jealous custodians of personal and spiritual spontaneity. They are indeed its only organized and recognized custodians in America to-day. They ought to guard against contributing to the increase of officialism and snobbery and insincerity as against a pestilence; they ought to keep truth and disinterested labor always in the foreground, treat degrees as secondary incidents, and in season and out of season make it plain that what they live for is to help men's souls, and not to decorate their persons with diplomas.

There seem to be three obvious ways in which the increasing hold of the Ph.D. Octopus upon American life can be kept in check.

The first way lies with the universities. They can lower their fantastic standards (which here at Harvard we are so proud of) and give the doctorate as a matter of course, just as they give the bachelor's degree, for a due amount of time spent in patient labor in a special department of learning, whether the man be a brilliantly gifted individual or not. Surely native distinction needs no official stamp, and should disdain to ask for one. On the other hand, faithful labor, however commonplace, and years devoted to a subject, always deserve to be acknowledged and requited.

The second way lies with both the universities and colleges. Let them give up their unspeakably silly ambition to bespangle their lists of officers with these doctorial titles Let them look more to substance and less to vanity and sham.

The third way lies with the individual student, and with his personal advisers in the faculties. Every man of native power, who might take a higher degree, and refuses to do so, because examinations interfere with the free following out of his more immediate intellectual aims, deserves well of his country, and in a rightly organized community, would not be made to suffer for his independence. With many men the passing of these extraneous tests is a very grievous interference indeed. Private letters of recommendation from their instructors, which in any event are ultimately needful, ought, in these cases, completely to offset the lack of the bread-winning degree; and instructors ought to be ready to advise students against it upon occasion, and to pledge themselves to back them later personally, in the market-struggle which they have to face.

It is indeed odd to see this love of titles —
and such titles — growing up in a country of
which the recognition of individuality and bare
manhood have so long been supposed to be
the very soul. The independence of the State,
in which most of our colleges stand, relieves
us of those more odious forms of academic
politics which continental European countries
present. Anything like the elaborate university machine of France, with its throttling influences upon individuals is unknown here.
The spectacle of the "Rath" distinction in
its innumerable spheres and grades, with
which all Germany is crawling to-day, is displeasing to American eyes; and displeasing
also in some respects is the institution of
knighthood in England, which, aping as it
does an aristocratic title, enables one's wife
as well as one's self so easily to dazzle the
servants at the house of one's friends. But
are we Americans ourselves destined after all
to hunger after similar vanities on an infinitely
more contemptible scale? And is individuality with us also going to count for nothing

unless stamped and licensed and authenticated by some title-giving machine? Let us pray that our ancient national genius may long preserve vitality enough to guard us from a future so unmanly and so unbeautiful!

II. THE TRUE HARVARD[1]

WHEN a man gets a decoration from a foreign institution, he may take it as an honor. Coming as mine has come to-day, I prefer to take it for that far more valuable thing, a token of personal good will from friends. Recognizing the good will and the friendliness, I am going to respond to the chairman's call by speaking exactly as I feel.

I am not an alumnus of the College. I have not even a degree from the Scientific School, in which I did some study forty years ago. I have no right to vote for Overseers, and I have never felt until to-day as if I were a child of the house of Harvard in the fullest sense. Harvard is many things in one — a school, a forcing house for thought, and also a social club; and the club aspect is so strong, the family tie so close and subtle among our Bachelors of Arts that all of us here who are

[1] Speech at the Harvard Commencement Dinner, June 24, 1903, after receiving an LL.D. degree. Printed in the *Graduates' Magazine* for September, 1903.

in my plight, no matter how long we may have lived here, always feel a little like outsiders on Commencement day. We have no class to walk with, and we often stay away from the procession. It may be foolish, but it is a fact. I don't believe that my dear friends Shaler, Hollis, Lanman, or Royce ever have felt quite as happy or as much at home as my friend Barrett Wendell feels upon a day like this.

I wish to use my present privilege to say a word for these outsiders with whom I belong. Many years ago there was one of them from Canada here — a man with a high-pitched voice, who could n't fully agree with all the points of my philosophy. At a lecture one day, when I was in the full flood of my eloquence, his voice rose above mine, exclaiming: "But, doctor, doctor! to be serious for a moment . . . ," in so sincere a tone that the whole room burst out laughing. I want you now to be serious for a moment while I say my little say. We are glorifying ourselves to-day, and whenever the name of

Harvard is emphatically uttered on such days, frantic cheers go up. There are days for affection, when pure sentiment and loyalty come rightly to the fore. But behind our mere animal feeling for old schoolmates and the Yard and the bell, and Memorial and the clubs and the river and the Soldiers' Field, there must be something deeper and more rational. There ought at any rate to be some possible ground in reason for one's boiling over with joy that one is a son of Harvard, and was not, by some unspeakably horrible accident of birth, predestined to graduate at Yale or at Cornell.

Any college can foster club loyalty of that sort. The only rational ground for pre-eminent admiration of any single college would be its pre-eminent spiritual tone. But to be a college man in the mere clubhouse sense — I care not of what college — affords no guarantee of real superiority in spiritual tone.

The old notion that book learning can be a panacea for the vices of society lies pretty well shattered to-day. I say this in spite of certain utterances of the President of this University to the teachers last year. That sanguine-hearted man seemed then to think that if the schools would only do their duty better, social vice might cease. But vice will never cease. Every level of culture breeds its own peculiar brand of it as surely as one soil breeds sugar-cane, and another soil breeds cranberries. If we were asked that disagreeable question, "What are the bosom-vices of the level of culture which our land and day have reached?" we should be forced, I think, to give the still more disagreeable answer that they are swindling and adroitness, and the indulgence of swindling and adroitness, and cant, and sympathy with cant — natural fruits of that extraordinary idealization of "success" in the mere outward sense of "getting there," and getting there on as big a scale as we can, which characterizes our present generation. What was Reason given to man for, some satirist has said, except to enable him to invent reasons for what he wants to do. We might say the same of education. We see college graduates on every side of every public question. Some of Tammany's stanchest supporters are Harvard men. Harvard men defend our treatment of our Filipino allies as a masterpiece of policy and morals. Harvard men, as journalists, pride themselves on producing copy for any side that may enlist them. There is not a public abuse for which some Harvard advocate may not be found.

In the successful sense, then, in the worldly sense, in the club sense, to be a college man, even a Harvard man, affords no sure guarantee for anything but a more educated cleverness in the service of popular idols and vulgar ends. Is there no inner Harvard within the outer Harvard which means definitively more than this — for which the outside men who come here in such numbers, come? They come from the remotest outskirts of our country, without introductions, without school affiliations; special students, scientific students, graduate students, poor students of the College, who make their living as they go. They seldom or never darken the doors of the Pudding or the Porcellian; they hover in the background on days when the crimson color is most in evidence, but they nevertheless are intoxicated and exultant with the nourishment they find here; and their loyalty is deeper and subtler and more a matter of the inmost soul than the gregarious loyalty of the clubhouse pattern often is.

Indeed, there is such an inner spiritual Harvard; and the men I speak of, and for whom I speak to-day, are its true missionaries and carry its gospel into infidel parts. When they come to Harvard, it is not primarily because she is a club. It is because they have heard of her persistently atomistic constitution, of her tolerance of exceptionality and eccentricity, of her devotion to the principles of individual vocation and choice. It is because you cannot make single one-ideaed regiments of her classes. It is because she cherishes so many vital ideals, yet makes a scale of value among them; so that even her apparently incurable second-rateness (or only

353

occasional first-rateness) in intercollegiate ath-
letics comes from her seeing so well that sport
is but sport, that victory over Yale is not the
whole of the law and the prophets, and that a
popgun is not the crack of doom.

The true Church was always the invisible
Church. The true Harvard is the invisible
Harvard in the souls of her more truth-seek-
ing and independent and often very solitary
sons. *Thoughts* are the precious seeds of
which our universities should be the botanical
gardens. Beware when God lets loose a
thinker on the world — either Carlyle or
Emerson said that — for all things then have
to rearrange themselves. But the thinkers
in their youth are almost always very lonely
creatures. "Alone the great sun rises and
alone spring the great streams." The university most worthy of rational admiration
is that one in which your lonely thinker can
feel himself least lonely, most positively
furthered, and most richly fed. On an occasion like this it would be poor taste to draw
comparisons between the colleges, and in

their mere clubhouse quality they cannot differ widely: — all must be worthy of the loyalties and affections they arouse. But as a nursery for independent and lonely thinkers I do believe that Harvard still is in the van. Here they find the climate so propitious that they can be happy in their very solitude. The day when Harvard shall stamp a single hard and fast type of character upon her children, will be that of her downfall. Our undisciplinables are our proudest product. Let us agree together in hoping that the output of them will never cease.

III. STANFORD'S IDEAL DESTINY[1]

FOREIGNERS, commenting on our civilization, have with great unanimity remarked the
privileged position that institutions of learning occupy in America as receivers of benefactions. Our typical men of wealth, if they
do not found a college, will at least single out
some college or university on which to lavish
legacies or gifts. All the more so, perhaps,
if they are not college-bred men themselves.
Johns Hopkins University, the University of
Chicago, Clark University, are splendid examples of this rule. Steadily, year by year,
my own university, Harvard, receives from
one to two and a half millions.

There is something almost pathetic in the
way in which our successful business men
seem to idealize the higher learning and to
believe in its efficacy for salvation. Never
having shared in its blessings, they do their
utmost to make the youth of coming genera-

[1] An Address at Stanford University on Founders'
Day, 1906. Printed in *Science*, for May 25, 1906.

tions more fortunate. Usually there is little originality of thought in their generous foundations. The donors follow the beaten track. Their good will has to be vague, for they lack the inside knowledge. What they usually think of is a new college like all the older colleges; or they give new buildings to a university or help to make it larger, without any definite idea as to the improvement of its inner form. Improvements in the character of our institutions always come from the genius of the various presidents and faculties. The donors furnish means of propulsion, the experts within the pale lay out the course and steer the vessel. You all think of the names of Eliot, Gilman, Hall and Harper as I utter these words — I mention no name nearer home.

This is founders' day here at Stanford — the day set apart each year to quicken and reanimate in all of us the consciousness of the deeper significance of this little university to which we permanently or temporarily belong. I am asked to use my voice to contribute to this effect. How can I do so better than by uttering quite simply and directly the impressions that I personally receive? I am one among our innumerable American teachers, reared on the Atlantic coast but admitted for this year to be one of the family at Stanford. I see things not wholly from without, as the casual visitor does, but partly from within. I am probably a typical observer. As my impressions are, so will be the impressions of others. And those impressions, taken together, will probably be the verdict of history on the institution which Leland and Jane Stanford founded.

"Where there is no vision, the people perish." Mr. and Mrs. Stanford evidently had a vision of the most prophetic sort. They saw the opportunity for an absolutely unique creation, they seized upon it with the boldness of great minds; and the passionate energy with which Mrs. Stanford after her husband's death, drove the original plans through in the face of every dismaying obstacle, forms a chapter in the biography of heroism. Heroic also the loyalty with which in those dark years the president and faculty made the university's cause, their cause, and shared the uncertainties and privations.

And what is the result to-day? To-day the key-note is triumphantly struck. The first step is made beyond recall. The character of the material foundation is assured for all time as something unique and unparalleled. It logically calls for an equally unique and unparalleled spiritual superstructure.

Certainly the chief impression which the existing university must make on every visitor is of something unique and unparalleled. Its attributes are almost too familiar to you to bear recapitulation. The classic scenery of its site, reminding one of Greece, Greek too in its atmosphere of opalescent fire, as if the hills that close us in were bathed in ether, milk and sunshine; the great city, near enough for convenience, too far ever to become invasive; the climate, so friendly to work that every morning wakes one fresh for new amounts of work; the noble archi-

tecture, so generously planned that there is
room and to spare for every requirement;
the democracy of the life, no one superflu-
ously rich, yet all sharing, so far as their
higher needs go, in the common endowment —
where could a genuis devoted to the search
for truth, and unworldly as most geniuses
are, find on the earth's whole round a place
more advantageous to come and work in?
Die Luft der Freiheit weht! All the traditions are individualistic. Red tape and organization are at their minimum. Interruptions
and perturbing distractions hardly exist.
Eastern institutions look all dark and huddled
and confused in comparison with this purity
and serenity. Shall it not be auspicious?
Surely the one destiny to which this happy
beginning seems to call Stanford is that it
should become something intense and original,
not necessarily in point of wealth or extent,
but in point of spiritual quality. The founders
have, as I said, triumphantly struck the key-
note, and laid the basis: the quality of what
they have already given is unique in character.

It rests with the officials of the present and future Stanford, it rests with the devotion and sympathetic insight of the growing body of graduates, to prolong the vision where the founders' vision terminated, and to insure that all the succeeding steps, like the first steps, shall single out this university more and more as the university of quality peculiarly.

And what makes essential quality in a university? Years ago in New England it was said that a log by the roadside with a student sitting on one end of it, and Mark Hopkins sitting on the other end, was a university. It is the quality of its men that makes the quality of a university. You may have your buildings, you may create your committees and boards and regulations, you may pile up your machinery of discipline and perfect your methods of instruction, you may spend money till no one can approach you; yet you will add nothing but one more trivial specimen to the common herd of American colleges, unless you send into all this organization some breath of life, by inoculating it with a few men, at least, who are real geniuses. And if you once have the geniuses, you can easily dispense with most of the organization. Like a contagious disease, almost, spiritual life passes from man to man by contact. Education in the long run is an affair that works itself out between the individual student and his opportunities. Methods of which we talk so much, play but a minor part. Offer the opportunities, leave the student to his natural reaction on them, and he will work out his personal destiny, be it a high one or a low one. Above all things, offer the opportunity of higher personal contacts. A university provides these anyhow within the student body, for it attracts the more aspiring of the youth of the country, and they befriend and elevate one another. But we are only beginning in this country, with our extraordinary American reliance on organization, to see that the alpha and omega in a university is the tone of it, and that this tone is set by human personalities exclusively.

The world, in fact, is only beginning to see that the wealth of a nation consists more than in anything else in the number of superior men that it harbors. In the practical realm it has always recognized this, and known that no price is too high to pay for a great statesman or great captain of industry. But it is equally so in the religious and moral sphere, in the poetic and artistic sphere and in the philosophic and scientific sphere. Geniuses are ferments; and when they come together as they have done in certain lands at certain times, the whole population seems to share in the higher energy which they awaken. The effects are incalculable and often not easy to trace in detail, but they are pervasive and momentous. Who can measure the effects on the national German soul of the splendid series of German poets and German men of learning, most of them academic personages?

From the bare economic point of view the importance of geniuses is only beginning to be appreciated. How can we measure the cash-value to France of a Pasteur, to England of a Kelvin, to Germany of an Ostwald, to us here of a Burbank? One main care of every country in the future ought to be to find out who its first-rate thinkers are and to help them. Cost here becomes something entirely irrelevant, the returns are sure to be so in-commensurable. This is what wise men the world over are perceiving. And as the universities are already a sort of agency providentially provided for the detection and encouragement of mental superiority, it would seem as if that one among them that followed this line most successfully would quickest rise to a position of paramountcy and distinction.

Why should not Stanford immediately adopt this as her vital policy? Her position is one of unprecedented freedom. Not trammelled by the service of the state as other universities on this coast are trammelled, independent of students' fees and consequently of numbers, utopian in the material respects I have enumerated, she only needs a boldness

364

like that shown by her founders to become the seat of a glowing intellectual life, sure to be admired and envied the world over. Let her claim her place; let her espouse her destiny. Let her call great investigators from whatever lands they live in, from England, France, Germany, Japan, as well as from America. She can do this without presumption, for the advantages of this place for steady mental work are so unparalleled. Let these men, following the happy traditions of the place, make the university. The original foundation had something eccentric in it; let Stanford not fear to be eccentric to the end, if need be. Let her not imitate; let her lead, not follow. Especially let her not be bound by vulgar traditions as to the cheapness or dearness of professorial service. The day is certainly about to dawn when some American university will break all precedents in the matter of instructors' salaries, and will thereby immediately take the lead, and reach the winning post for quality. I like to think of Stanford being that university. Geniuses are sensitive plants, in some respects like *prima donnas*. They have to be treated tenderly. They don't need to live in superfluity; but they need freedom from harassing care; they need books and instruments; they are always overworking, so they need generous vacations; and above all things they need occasionally to travel far and wide in the interests of their souls' development. Where quality is the thing sought after, the thing of supreme quality is cheap, whatever be the price one has to pay for it.

Considering all the conditions, the quality of Stanford has from the first been astonishingly good both in the faculty and in the student body. Can we not, as we sit here to-day, frame a vision of what it may be a century hence, with the honors of the intervening years all rolled up in its traditions? Not vast, but intense; less a place for teaching youths and maidens than for training scholars; devoted to truth; radiating influence; setting standards; shedding abroad the fruits of learning; mediating between America and

Asia, and helping the more intellectual men of both continents to understand each other better.

What a history! and how can Stanford ever fail to enter upon it?

XV

A PLURALISTIC MYSTIC

XV

A PLURALISTIC MYSTIC[1]

Nor for the ignoble vulgar do I write this article, but only for those dialectic-mystic souls who have an irresistible taste, acquired or native, for higher flights of metaphysics. I have always held the opinion that one of the first duties of a good reader is to summon other readers to the enjoyment of any un-known author of rare quality whom he may discover in his explorations. Now for years my own taste, literary as well as philosophic, has been exquisitely titillated by a writer the name of whom I think must be unknown to the readers of this article; so I no longer continue silent about the merits of Benjamin Paul Blood.

Mr. Blood inhabits a city otherwise, I imagine, quite unvisited by the Muses, the

· [1] Written during the early summer of 1910 and published in the *Hibbert Journal* for July of that year.

371

town called Amsterdam, situated on the New York Central Railroad. What his regular or bread-winning occupation may be I know not, but it can't have made him super-wealthy. He is an author only when the fit strikes him, and for short spurts at a time; shy, moreover, to the point of publishing his compositions only as private tracts, or in letters to such far-from-reverberant organs of publicity as the *Gazette* or the *Recorder* of his native Amsterdam, or the *Utica Herald* or the *Albany Times*. Odd places for such subtile efforts to appear in, but creditable to American editors in these degenerate days! Once, indeed, the lamented W. T. Harris of the old "Journal of Speculative Philosophy" got wind of these epistles, and the result was a revision of some of them for that review (*Philosophic Reveries*, 1889). Also a couple of poems were reprinted from their leaflets by the editor of *Scribner's Magazine* ("The Lion of the Nile," 1888, and "Nemesis," 1899). But apart from these three dashes before the footlights, Mr. Blood has kept behind the curtain all his days.[1]

The author's maiden adventure was the *Anæsthetic Revelation,* a pamphlet printed privately at Amsterdam in 1874. I forget how it fell into my hands, but it fascinated me so "weirdly" that I am conscious of its having been one of the stepping-stones of my thinking ever since. It gives the essence of Blood's philosophy, and shows most of the features of his talent — albeit one finds in it little humor and no verse. It is full of verbal felicity, felicity sometimes of precision, sometimes of metaphoric reach; it begins with dialectic reasoning, of an extremely Fichtean and Hegelian type, but it ends in a trumpet-blast of oracular mysticism, straight from the insight wrought by anæsthetics — of all things

[1] "Yes! Paul is quite a correspondent!" said a good citizen of Amsterdam, from whom I inquired the way to Mr. Blood's dwelling many years ago, after alighting from the train. I had sought to identify him by calling him an "author," but his neighbor thought of him only as a writer of letters to the journals I have named.

in the world — and unlike anything one ever heard before. The practically unanimous tradition of "regular" mysticism has been unquestionably *monistic;* and inasmuch as it is the characteristic of mystics to speak, not as the scribes, but as men who have "been there" and seen with their own eyes, I think that this sovereign manner must have made some other pluralistic-minded students hesitate, as I confess that it has often given pause to me. One cannot criticise the vision of a mystic — one can but pass it by, or else accept it as having some amount of evidential weight. I felt unable to do either with a good conscience until I met with Mr. Blood. His mysticism, which may, if one likes, be understood as monistic in this earlier utterance, develops in the later ones a sort of "left-wing" voice of defiance, and breaks into what to my ear has a radically pluralistic sound. I confess that the existence of this novel brand of mysticism has made my cowering mood depart. I feel now as if my own pluralism were not without the kind of support

374

which mystical corroboration may confer. Morrison can no longer claim to be the only beneficiary of whatever right mysticism may possess to lend *prestige*.

This is my philosophic, as distinguished from my literary, interest, in introducing Mr. Blood to this more fashionable audience: his philosophy, however mystical, is in the last resort not dissimilar from my own. I must treat him by "extracting" him, and simplify — certainly all too violently — as I extract. He is not consecutive as a writer, aphoristic and oracular rather; and being moreover sometimes dialectic, sometimes poetic, and sometimes mystic in his manner; sometimes monistic and sometimes pluralistic in his matter, I have to run my own risk in making him orate *pro domo mea*, and I am not quite unprepared to hear him say, in case he ever reads these pages, that I have entirely missed his point. No matter; I will proceed.

I

I will separate his diverse phases and take him first as a pure dialectician. Dialectic thought of the Hegelian type is a whirlpool into which some persons are sucked out of the stream which the straightforward understanding follows. Once in the eddy, nothing but rotary motion can go on. All who have been in it know the feel of its swirl — they know thenceforward that thinking unreturning on itself is but one part of reason, and that rectilinear mentality, in philosophy at any rate, will never do. Though each one may report in different words of his rotational experience, the experience itself is almost childishly simple, and whosoever has been there instantly recognizes other authentic reports. To have been in that eddy is a freemasonry of which the common password is a "fie" on all the operations of the simple popular understanding.

In Hegel's mind the vortex was at its liveliest, and any one who has dipped into

Hegel will recognize Mr. Blood to be of the same tribe. "That Hegel was pervaded by the great truth," Blood writes, "cannot be doubted. The eyes of philosophy, if not set directly on him, are set towards the region which he occupied. Though he may not be the final philosopher, yet pull him out, and all the rest will be drawn into his vacancy."

Drawn into the same whirlpool, Mr. Blood means. Non-dialectic thought takes facts as singly given, and accounts for one fact by another. But when we think of "*all* fact," we see that nothing of the nature of fact can explain it, "for that were but one more added to the list of things to be accounted for. . . . The beginning of curiosity, in the philosophic sense," Mr. Blood again writes, "is the stare of being at itself, in the wonder why anything is at all, and what this being signifies. Naturally we first assume the void, and then wonder how, with no ground and no fertility, anything should come into it." We treat it as a positive nihility, "a barrier from which all our batted balls of being rebound."

Upon this idea Mr. Blood passes the usual transcendentalist criticism. There *is* no such separate opposite to being; yet we never think of being as such — of pure being as distinguished from specific forms of being — save as what stands relieved against this imaginary background. Being has no *outline* but that which non-being makes, and the two ideas form an inseparable pair. "Each limits and defines the other. Either would be the other in the same position, for here (where there is as yet no question of content, but only of being itself) the position is all and the content is nothing. Hence arose that paradox: 'Being is by nothing more real than not-being.'"

"Popularly," Mr. Blood goes on, "we think of all that is as having got the better of non-being. If all were not — *that*, we think, were easy: there were no wonder then, no tax on ingenuity, nothing to be accounted for. This conclusion is from the thinking which assumes all reality as immediately given, assumes knowledge as a simple physical light, rather than as a distinction involving light and darkness equally. We assume that if the light were to go out, the show would be ended (and so it would); but we forget that if the darkness were to go out, that would be equally calamitous. It were bad enough if the master had lost his crayon, but the loss of the blackboard would be just as fatal to the demonstration. Without darkness light would be useless — universal light as blind as universal darkness. Universal thing and universal no-thing were indistinguishable. Why, then, assume the positive, the immediately affirmative, as alone the ingenious? Is not the mould as shapely as the model? The original ingenuity does not show in bringing light out of darkness, nor in bringing things out of nothing, but in evolving, through the just opposition of light and darkness, this wondrous picture, in which the black and white lines have equal significance — in evolving from life and death at once, the conscious spirit. . . .

"It is our habit to think of life as dear,

and of death as cheap (though Tithonus found them otherwise), or, continuing the simile of the picture, that paper is cheap while drawing is expensive; but the engraver had a different estimation in one sense, for all his labor was spent on the white ground, while he left untouched those parts of the block which make the lines in the picture. If being and non-being are both necessary to the presence of either, neither shall claim priority or preference. Indeed, we may fancy an intelligence which, instead of regarding things as simply owning entity, should regard chiefly their background as affected by the holes which things are making in it. Even so, the paper-maker might see your picture as intrusive!"

Thus "does the negation of being appear as indispensable in the making of it." But to anyone who should appeal to particular forms of being to refute this paradox, Mr. Blood admits that "to say that a picture, or any other sensuous thing, is the same as the want of it, were to utter nonsense indeed:

there is a difference equivalent to the whole stuff and merit of the picture; but in so far as the picture can be there for thought, as something either asserted or negated, its presence or its absence are the same and indifferent. By *its* absence we do not mean the absence of anything else, nor absence in general; and how, forsooth, does its absence differ from these other absences, save by containing a complete description of the picture? The hole is as round as the plug; and from our thought the 'picture' cannot get away. The negation is specific and descriptive, and what it destroys it preserves for our conception."

The result is that, whether it be taken generally or taken specifically, all that which *either is or is not* is or is not *by distinction or opposition*. "And observe the life, the process, through which this slippery doubleness endures. Let us suppose the present tense, that gods and men and angels and devils march all abreast in this present instant, and the only real time and date in the universe is

now. And what *is* this instant now? Whatever else, it is *process* — becoming and departing; with what between? Simply division,
difference; the present has no breadth for
if it had, that which we seek would be the
middle of that breadth. There is no precipitate, as on a stationary platform, of the process of becoming, no residuum of the process
of departing, but between the two is a curtain,
the apparition of difference, which is all the
world."

I am using my scissors somewhat at random
on my author's paragraphs, since one place
is as good as another for entering a ring by,
and the expert reader will discern at once the
authentic dialectic circling. Other paragraphs
show Mr. Blood as more Hegelian still, and
thoroughly idealistic: —

"Assume that knowing is distinguishing,
and that distinction is of difference; if one
knows a difference, one knows it as of entities
which afford it, and which also he knows;
and he must know the entities and the difference apart, — one from the other. Knowing

all this, he should be able to answer the twin question, 'What is the difference *between sameness and difference?*' It is a 'twin' question, because the two terms are equal in the proposition, and each is full of the other. . . .

"Sameness has 'all the difference in the world' — from difference; and difference is an entity as difference — it being identically that. They are alike and different at once, since either is the other when the observer would contrast it with the other; so that the sameness and the difference are 'subjective,' are the property of the observer: his is the 'limit' in their unlimited field. . . .

"We are thus apprized that distinction involves and carries its own identity; and that ultimate distinction — distinction in the last analysis — is self-distinction , 'self-knowledge,' as we realize it consciously every day. Knowledge is self-referred: to know is to know that you know, and to be known as well.

" 'Ah! but *both in the same time ?*' inquires the logician. A subject-object knowing itself as a seamless unit, while yet its two items

383

show a real distinction: this passes all understanding."

But the whole of idealism goes to the proof
that the two sides *cannot* succeed one another
in a time-process. "To say you know, and
you know that you know, is to add nothing
in the last clause; it is as idle as to say that
you lie, and you know that you lie," for if
you know it not you lie not.

Philosophy seeks to grasp totality, "but
the power of grasping or consenting to totality involves the power of thought to make
itself its own object. Totality itself may
indeed be taken by the *naïve* intellect as an
immediate topic, in the sense of being just
an *object*, but it cannot be just that; for the
knower, as other or opposite, would still be
within that totality. The 'universe' by definition must contain all opposition. If distinction should vanish, what would remain?
To what other could it change as a whole?
How can the loss of distinction make a
difference? Any loss, at its utmost, offers
a new status with the old, but obviously it

A PLURALISTIC MYSTIC

is too late now to efface distinction by a
change. There is no possible conjecture, but
such as carries with it the subjective that
holds it; and when the conjecture is of distinction in general, the subjective fills the
void with distinction of itself. The ultimate,
ineffaceable distinction is self-distinction,
self-consciousness. . . . 'Thou art the unan-
swered question, couldst see thy proper eye.'
. . . The thought that must be is the very
thought of our experience; the ultimate
opposition, the to be *and* not to be, is personality, spirit — somewhat that is in knowing that it is, and is nothing else but this
knowing in its vast relations. [1]

[1] "How shall a man know he is alive — since in
thought the knowing constitutes the being alive, without knowing that thought (life) from its opposite, and
so knowing both, and so far as being is knowing, being
both? Each defines and relieves the other, each is
impossible in thought without the other; therefore
each has no distinction save as presently contrasting
with the other, and each by itself is the same, and nothing. Clearly, then, consciousness is neither of one nor
of the other nor of bóth, but a knowing subject perceiving them and itself together and as one. . . . So,
in coming out of the anæsthetic exhilaration . . . we

"Here lies the bed-rock; here the brain-sweat of twenty-five centuries crystallizes to a jewel five words long: 'The Universe has No Opposite.' For there the wonder of that which is, rests safe in the perception that all things *are* only through the opposition which is their only fear."

"The inevitable generally," in short, is exactly and identically that which in point of fact is actually here.

This is the familiar nineteenth-century development of Kant's idealistic vision. To me it sounds monistic enough to charm the monist in me unreservedly. I listen to the

want to tell something; but the effort instantly proves that something will stay back and do the telling — one must utter one's own throat, one must eat one's own teeth, to express the being that possesses one. The result is ludicrous and astounding at once — astounding in the clear perception that this is the ultimate mystery of life, and is given you as the old Adamic secret, which you then feel that all intelligence must sometime know or have known; yet ludicrous in its familiar simplicity, as somewhat that any man should always perceive at his best, if his head were only level, but which in our ordinary thinking has grown into a thousand creeds and theories dignified as religion and philosophy."

felicitously-worded   concept-music . circling
round itself, as on some drowsy summer
noon one listens under the pines to the
murmuring of leaves and insects, and with
as little thought of criticism.

But Mr. Blood strikes a still more vibrant
note: "No more can be than rationally is;
and this was always true.   There is no reason
for what is not; but for what there is reason,
that *is* and. ever was.   Especially is there no
becoming of reason, and hence no reason for
becoming, to a sufficient intelligence.   In the
sufficient intelligence all things always are,
and are rational.   To say there is something
yet to be which never was, not even in the
sufficient intelligence wherein the world is
rational and not a blind and orphan waif,
is to ignore all reason.   Aught that might be
assumed as contingently coming to be could
only have 'freedom' for its origin; and
'freedom' has not fertility or invention, and
is not a reason for any special thing, but the
very vacuity of a ground for anything in
preference to its room.   Neither is there in

bare time any principle or originality whereby anything should come or go. . . .

"Such idealism enures greatly to the dignity and repose of man. No blind fate, prior to what is, shall necessitate that all first be and afterward be known, but knowledge is first, with fate in her own hands. When we are depressed by the weight and immensity of the immediate, we find in idealism a wondrous consolation. The alien positive, so vast and overwhelming by itself, reduces its pretensions when the whole negative confronts it on our side.[1] It matters little for its greatness when an equal greatness is opposed. When one remembers that the balance and motion of the planets are so delicate that the momentary scowl of an eclipse may fill the heavens with tempest, and even affect the very bowels

[1] Elsewhere Mr. Blood writes of the "force of the negative" thus: — "As when a faded lock of woman's hair shall cause a man to cut his throat in a bedroom at five o'clock in the morning; or when Albany resounds with legislation, but a little henpecked judge in a dusty office at Herkimer or Johnstown sadly writes across the page the word 'unconstitutional' — the glory of the Capitol has faded."

of the earth — when we see a balloon, that
carries perhaps a thousand pounds, leap up
a hundred feet at the discharge of a sheet of
note paper — or feel it stand deathly still in
a hurricane, because it goes with the hurricane, sides with it, and ignores the rushing
world below — we should realize that one
tittle of pure originality would outweigh this
crass objective, and turn these vast masses
into mere breath and tissue-paper show." [1]

---

[1] Elsewhere Blood writes: — "But what then, in
the name of common sense, *is* the external world? If a
dead man could answer he would say Nothing, or as
Macbeth said of the air-drawn dagger, 'there is no such
thing.' But a live man's answer might be in this way:
What is the multiplication table when it is not written
down? It is a necessity of thought; it was not created,
it cannot but be; every intelligence which goes to it,
and thinks, must think in that form or think falsely.
So the universe is the static necessity of reason; it is
not an object for any intelligence to find, but it is half
object and half subject; it never cost anything as a
whole; it never *was* made, but always *is* made, in the
Logos, or expression of reason — the Word; and
slowly but surely it will be understood and uttered in
every intelligence, until he is one with God or reason
itself. As a man, for all he knows, or has known,
stands at any given instant the realization of only one
thought, while all the rest of him is invisibly linked to

389

But whose is the originality? There is nothing in what I am treating as this phase of our author's thought to separate it from the old-fashioned rationalism. There must be a reason for every fact; and so much reason, so fact. The reason is always the whole foil and background and negation of the fact, the whole remainder of reality. "A man may feel good only by feeling better. . . . Pleasure is ever in the company and contrast of pain; for instance, in thirsting and drinking, the pleasure of the one is the exact measure of the pain of the other, and they cease precisely together — otherwise the patient would drink more. The black and yellow gonfalon of Lucifer is indispensable in any spiritual picture." Thus do truth's two components seem to balance, vibrating across the centre of indifference; "being and

that in the necessary form and concatenation of reason, so the man as a whole of exploited thoughts is a moment in the front of the concatenated reason of the universal whole; and this whole is personal only as it is personally achieved. This is the Kingdom that is 'within you,' and the *God* which 'no man hath seen at any time.'"

non-being have equal value and cost," and "mainly are convertible in their terms." [1]

This sounds radically monistic; and monistic also is the first account of the Ether-revelation, in which we read that "thenceforth each is all, in God. . . . The One remains,

[1] There are passages in Blood that sound like a well-known essay by Emerson. For instance: — "Experience burns into us the fact and the necessity of universal compensation. The philosopher takes it from Heraclitus, in the insight that everything exists through its opposite; and the bummer comforts himself for his morning headache as only the rough side of a square deal. We accept readily the doctrine that pain and pleasure, evil and good, death and life, chance and reason, are necessary equations — that there must be just as much of each as of its other.

"It grieves us little that this great compensation cannot at every instant balance its beam on every individual centre, and dispense with an under dog in every fight; we know that the parts must subserve the whole; we have faith that our time will come; and if it comes not at all in this world, our lack is a bid for immortality, and the most promising argument for a world hereafter. 'Though He slay me, yet will I trust in Him.'

"This is the faith that baffles all calamity, and ensures genius and patience in the world. Let not the creditor hasten the settlement: let not the injured man hurry toward revenge; there is nothing that draws bigger interest than a wrong, and to 'get the best of it' is ever in some sense to get the worst."

391

the many change and pass; and every one of us is the One that remains."

II

It seems to me that any transcendental idealist who reads this article ought to discern in the fragmentary utterances which I have quoted thus far, the note of what he considers the truer dialectic profundity. He ought to extend the glad hand of fellowship to Mr. Blood; and if he finds him afterwards palavering with the enemy, he ought to count him, not as a simple ignoramus or Philistine, but as a renegade and relapse. He cannot possibly be treated as one who sins because he never has known better, or as one who walks in darkness because he is congenitally blind.

Well, Mr. Blood, explain it as one may, does turn towards the darkness as if he had never seen the light. Just listen for a moment to such irrationalist deliverances on his part as these: —

"Reason is neither the first nor the last

word in this world. Reason is an equation; it gives but a pound for a pound. Nature is excess; she is evermore, without cost or explanation.

> ' Is heaven so poor that *justice*
>   Metes the bounty of the skies?
> So poor that every blessing
>   Fills the debit of a cost?
> That all process is returning?
>   And all gain is of the lost? '

Go back into reason, and you come at last to fact, nothing more — a given-ness, a something to wonder at and yet admit, like your own will. And all these tricks for logicizing originality, self-relation, absolute process, subjective contradiction, will wither in the breath of the mystical fact; they will swirl down the corridors before the besom of the everlasting Yea."

Or again: "The monistic notion of a oneness, a centred wholeness, ultimate purpose, or climacteric result of the world, has wholly given way. Thought evolves no longer a centred whole, a One, but rather a numberless many, adjust it how we will."

Or still again: "The pluralists have talked philosophy to a standstill — Nature is contingent, excessive and mystical essentially."

Have we here contradiction simply, a man converted from one faith to its opposite? Or is it only dialectic circling, like the opposite points on the rim of a revolving disc, one moving up, one down, but replacing one another endlessly, while the whole disc never moves? If it be this latter — Mr. Blood himself uses the image — the dialectic is too pure for me to catch: a deeper man must mediate the monistic with the pluralistic Blood. Let my incapacity be castigated, if my "Subject" ever reads this article, but let me treat him from now onwards as the simply pluralistic mystic which my reading of the rest of him suggests. I confess to some dread of my own fate at his hands. In making so far an ordinary transcendental idealist of him, I have taken liberties, running separate sentences together, inverting their order, and even altering single words, for all which I beg pardon; but in treating my author from now onwards as a pluralist, interpretation is easier, and my hands can be less stained (if they *are* stained) with exegetic blood.

I have spoken of his verbal felicity, and alluded to his poetry. Before passing to his mystic gospel, I will refresh the reader (doubtless now fatigued with so much dialectic) by a sample of his verse. "The Lion of the Nile" is an allegory of the "champion spirit of the world" in its various incarnations.

Thus it begins:—

"Whelped on the desert sands, and desert bred
  From dugs whose sustenance was blood alone—
  A life translated out of other lives,
  I grew the king of beasts; the hurricane
  Leaned like a feather on my royal fell;
  I took the Hyrcan tiger by the scruff
  And tore him piecemeal; my hot bowels laughed
  And my fangs yearned for prey. Earth was my
        lair:
  I slept on the red desert without fear:
  I roamed the jungle depths with less design
  Than e'en to lord their solitude; on crags
  That cringe from lightning—black and blasted
        fronts
  That crouch beneath the wind-bleared stars, I told

395

My heart's fruition to the universe,
And all night long, roaring my fierce defy,
I thrilled the wilderness with aspen terrors,
And challenged death and life. . . ."

Again:

"Naked I stood upon the raked arena
Beneath the pennants of Vespasian,
While seried thousands gazed — strangers from
    Caucasus,
Men of the Grecian Isles, and Barbary princes,
To see me grapple with the counterpart
Of that I had been — the raptorial jaws,
The arms that wont to crush with strength alone,
The eyes that glared vindictive. — Fallen there,
Vast wings upheaved me; from the Alpine peaks
Whose avalanches swirl the valley mists
And whelm the helpless cottage, to the crown
Of Chimborazo, on whose changeless jewels
The torrid rays recoil, with ne'er a cloud
To swathe their blistered steps, I rested not,
But preyed on all that ventured from the earth,
An outlaw of the heavens. — But evermore
Must death release me to the jungle shades;
And there like Samson's grew my locks again
In the old walks and ways, till scapeless fate
Won me as ever to the haunts of men,
Luring my lives with battle and with love." . . .

I quote less than a quarter of the poem, of
which the rest is just as good, and I ask: Who

of us all handles his English vocabulary better than Mr. Blood? [1]

His proclamations of the mystic insight have a similar verbal power: —

"There is an invariable and reliable condition (or uncondition) ensuing about the instant of recall from anæsthetic stupor to 'coming to,' in which the genius of being is revealed. . . . No words may express the imposing certainty of the patient that he is realizing the primordial Adamic surprise of Life.

"Repetition of the experience finds it ever the same, and as if it could not possibly be otherwise. The subject resumes his normal consciousness only to partially and fitfully

[1] Or what thinks the reader of the verbiage of these verses? — addressed in a mood of human defiance to the cosmic Gods —

" Whose lightnings tawny leap from furtive lairs,
To helpless murder, while the ships go down
Swirled in the crazy stound, and mariners' prayers
Go up in noisome bubbles — such to *them;*—
Or when they tramp about the central fires,
Bending the strata with æonian tread
Till steeples totter, and all ways are lost, —
Deem they of wife or child, or home or friend,
Doing these things as the long years lead on
Only to other years that mean no more,
That cure no ill, nor make for use or proof —
Destroying ever, though to rear again."

remember its occurrence, and to try to formulate its baffling import, — with but this consolatory afterthought: that he has known the oldest truth, and that he has done with human theories as to the origin, meaning, or destiny of the race. He is beyond instruction in 'spiritual things.' . . .

"It is the instant contrast of this 'tasteless water of souls' with formal thought as we 'come to,' that leaves in the patient an astonishment that the awful mystery of Life is at last but a homely and a common thing, and that aside from mere formality the majestic and the absurd are of equal dignity. The astonishment is aggravated as at a thing of course, missed by sanity in overstepping, as in too foreign a search, or with too eager an attention: as in finding one's spectacles on one's nose, or in making in the dark a step higher than the stair. My first experiences of this revelation had many varieties of emotion; but as a man grows calm and determined by experience in general, so am I now not only firm and familiar in this once weird condition, but triumphant, divine. To minds of sanguine imagination there will be a sadness in the tenor of the mystery, as if the key-note of the universe were low; for no poetry, no emotion known to the normal sanity of man, can furnish a hint of its primeval prestige, and its all-but appalling solemnity; but for such as have felt sadly the instability of temporal things there is a comfort of serenity and ancient peace; while for the resolved and imperious spirit there are majesty and supremacy unspeakable. Nor can it be long until all who enter the anæsthetic condition (and there are hundreds every secular day) will be taught to expect this revelation, and will date from its experience their initiation into the Secret of Life. . . .

"This has been my moral sustenance since I have known of it. In my first printed mention of it I declared: 'The world is no more the alien terror that was taught me. Spurning the cloud-grimed and still sultry battlements whence so lately Jehovan thunders boomed, my gray gull lifts her wing against the night fall, and takes the dim leagues with a fearless eye.' And now, after twenty-seven years of this experience, the wing is grayer, but the eye is fearless still, while I renew and doubly emphasize that declaration. I know, as having known, the meaning of Existence; the sane centre of the universe — at once the wonder and the assurance of the soul."

After this rather literary interlude I return to Blood's philosophy again. I spoke a while ago of its being an "irrationalistic" philosophy in its latest phase. Behind every "fact" rationalism postulates its "reason." Blood parodizes this demand in true nominalistic fashion. "The goods are not enough, but they must have the invoice with them. There must be a *name*, something *to read*. I think of Dickens's horse that always fell down when they took him out of the shafts; or of the fellow who felt weak when naked, but strong in his overcoat." No bad mockery, this, surely, of rationalism's habit of explaining things by putting verbal doubles of them beneath them as their ground!

"All that philosophy has sought as cause, or reason," he says, "pluralism subsumes in the status and the given fact, where it stands as plausible as it may ever hope to stand. There may be disease in the presence of a question as well as in the lack of an answer. We do not wonder so strangely at an ingenious and well-set-up effect, for we feel such in ourselves; but a cause, reaching out beyond the verge [of fact] and dangling its legs in nonentity, with the hope of a rational foothold, should realize a strenuous life. Pluralism believes in truth and reason, but only as mystically realized, as lived in experience. Up from the breast of a man, up to his tongue and brain, comes a free and strong determination, and he cries, originally, and in spite of his whole nature and environment, 'I will.' This is the Jovian *fiat*, the pure cause. This is reason; this or nothing shall explain the world for him. For how shall he entertain a reason bigger than himself? . . . Let a man stand fast, then, as an axis of the earth; the obsequious meridians will bow to him, and gracious latitudes will measure from his feet."

This seems to be Blood's mystical answer to his own monistic statement which I quoted above, that "freedom" has no fertility, and is no reason for any special thing.[1] "Philo-

[1] I subjoin a poetic apostrophe of Mr. Blood's to freedom:

> "Let it ne'er be known.
> If in some book of the Inevitable,
> Dog-eared and stale, the future stands engrossed
> E'en as the past. There shall be news in heaven,
> And question in the courts thereof; and chance
> Shall have its fling, e'en at the [ermined] bench.
>
>   .   .   .   .
>
>   Ah, long ago, above the Indian ocean,
> Where wan stars brood over the dreaming East,
> I saw, white, liquid, palpitant, the Cross;
> And faint and far came bells of Calvary
> As planets passed, singing that they were saved,
> Saved from themselves: but ever low Orion —
> For hunter too was I, born of the wild,
> And the game flavor of the infinite
> Tainted me to the bône — he waved me on,
> On to the tangent field beyond all orbs,
> Where form nor order nor continuance
> Hath thought nor name; there unity exhales
> In want of confine, and the protoplasm
> May beat and beat, in aimless vehemence,
> Through vagrant spaces, homeless and unknown.
>
>   .   .   .   .
>
>   There ends One's empire! — but so ends not all;
> One knows not all; my griefs at least are mine —
> By me their measure, and to me their lesson;
> E'en I am one — (poor deuce to call the Ace!)
> And to the open bears my gonfalon,
> Mine ægis, Freedom! — Let me ne'er look back
> Accusing, for the withered leaves and lives

sophy," Mr. Blood writes to me in a letter, "is past. It was the long endeavor to logicize what we can only realize practically or in immediate experience. I am more and more impressed that Heraclitus insists on the equation of reason and unreason, or chance, as well as of being and not-being, etc. This throws the secret beyond logic, and makes mysticism outclass philosophy. The insight that mystery, — the Mystery, as such is final, is the hymnic word. If you use reason pragmatically, and deny it absolutely, you can't be beaten; be assured of that. But the *Fact* remains, and of course the Mystery." [1]

> The sated past hath strewn, the shears of fate,
> But forth to braver days.
> > O, Liberty,
> Burthen of every sigh! — thou gold of gold,
> Beauty of the beautiful, strength of the strong!
> My soul for ever turns agaze for thee.
> There is no purpose of eternity
> For faith or patience; but thy buoyant torch
> Still lighted from the Islands of the Blest,
> O'erbears all present for potential heavens
> Which are not — ah, so more than all that are!
> Whose chance postpones the ennui of the skies!
> Be thou my genius — be my hope in thee!
> For this were heaven: to be, and to be free."

[1] In another letter Mr. Blood writes:—"I think we are through with 'the Whole,' and with '*causa sui*,' and with the 'negative unity' which assumes to iden-

The "Fact," as I understand the writer here to mean it, remains in its native disseminated shape. From every realized amount of fact some other fact is *absent*, as being uninvolved. "There is nowhere more of it consecutively, perhaps, than appears upon this present page." There is, indeed, to put it otherwise, no more one all-enveloping fact than there is one all-enveloping spire in an endlessly growing spiral, and no more one all-generating fact than there is one central point in which an endlessly converging spiral ends. Hegel's "bad infinite" belongs to the eddy as well as to the line. "Progress?" writes our author. "And to what? Time turns a weary and a wistful face; has he not traversed an eternity? and shall another give

tify each thing as being what it lacks of everything else. You can, of course, build out a chip by modelling the sphere it was chipped from; — but if it was n't a sphere? What a weariness it is to look back over the twenty odd volumes of the ' Journal of Speculative Philosophy ' and see Harris's mind wholly filled by that one conception of self-determination — everything to be thought as 'part of a system' — a 'whole' and '*causa sui*.' — I should like to see such an idea get into the head of Edison or George Westinghouse."

the secret up? We have dreamed of a climax
and a consummation, a final triumph where a
world shall burn *en barbecue;* but there is
not, cannot be, a purpose of eternity; it
shall pay mainly as it goes, or not at all. The
show is on; and what a show, if we will but
give our attention! Barbecues, bonfires, and
banners? Not twenty worlds a minute would
keep up our bonfire of the sun; and what
banners of our fancy could eclipse the meteor
pennants of the pole, or the opaline splen-
dors of the everlasting ice? . . . Doubtless
we *are* ostensibly progressing, but there have
been prosperity and highjinks before. Nin-
eveh and Tyre, Rome, Spain, and Venice also
had their day. We are going, but it is a question of our standing the pace. It would seem
that the news must become less interesting
or tremendously more so — 'a breath can
make us, as a breath has made.'"

Elsewhere we read: "Variety, not unifor-
mity, is more likely to be the key to progress.
The genius of being is whimsical rather than
consistent. Our strata show broken bones

405

of histories all forgotten. How can it be otherwise? There can be no purpose of eternity. It is process all. The most sublime result, if it appeared as the ultimatum, would go stale in an hour; it could not be endured."

Of course from an intellectual point of view this way of thinking must be classed as scepticism. "Contingency forbids any inevitable history, and conclusions are absurd. Nothing in Hegel has kept the planet from being blown to pieces." Obviously the mystical "security," the "apodal sufficiency" yielded by the anæsthetic revelation, are very different moods of mind from aught that rationalism can claim to father — more active, prouder, more heroic. From his ether-intoxication Blood may feel towards ordinary rationalists "as Clive felt towards those millions of Orientals in whom honor had no part." On page 6, above, I quoted from his "Nemesis" — "Is heaven so poor that justice," etc. The writer goes on, addressing the goddess of "compensation" or rational balance: —

"How shalt thou poise the courage
  That covets all things hard?
How pay the love unmeasured
  That could not brook reward?
How prompt self-loyal honor
  Supreme above desire,
That bids the strong die for the weak,
  The martyrs sing in fire?
Why do I droop in bower
  And sigh in sacred hall?
Why stifle under shelter?
  Yet where, through forest tall,
The breath of hungry winter
  In stinging spray resolves,
I sing to the north wind's fury
  And shout with the coarse-haired wolves?

. . . .

What of thy priests' confuting,
  Of fate and form and law,
Of being and essence and counterpoise,
  Of poles that drive and draw?
Ever some compensation,
  Some pandering purchase still!
But the vehm of achieving reason
  Is the all-patrician Will!"

Mr. Blood must manage to re-write the
last two lines; but the contrast of the two
securities, his and the rationalist's, is plain

enough. The rationalist sees safe conditions. But Mr. Blood's revelation, whatever the conditions be, helps him to stand ready for a life among them. In this, his attitude seems to resemble that of Nietzsche's *amor fati!* "Simply," he writes to me, "*we do not know. But when we say we do not know, we are not to say it weakly and meekly, but with confidence and content. . . .* Knowledge is and must ever be *secondary*, a witness rather than a principal, or a 'principle'! — in the case. Therefore mysticism for me!"

"Reason," he prints elsewhere, "is but an item in the duplex potency of the mystery, and behind the proudest consciousness that ever reigned, Reason and Wonder blushed face to face. The legend sinks to burlesque if in that great argument which antedates man and his mutterings, Lucifer had not a fighting chance. . . .

"It is given to the writer and to others for whom he is permitted to speak — and we are grateful that it is the custom of gentlemen to believe one another — that the highest thought is not a milk-and-water equation of so much reason and so much result — 'no school sum to be cast up.' We have realized the highest divine thought of itself, and there is in it as much of wonder as of certainty; inevitable, and solitary and safe in one sense, but queer and cactus-like no less in another sense, it appeals unutterably to experience alone.

"There are sadness and disenchantment for the novice in these inferences, as if the key-note of the universe were low, but experience will approve them. Certainty is the root of despair. The inevitable stales, while doubt and hope are sisters. Not unfortunately the universe is wild — game flavored as a hawk's wing. Nature is miracle all. She knows no laws; the same returns not, save to bring the different. The slow round of the engraver's lathe gains but the breadth of a hair, but the difference is distributed back over the whole curve, never an instant true — ever not quite."

"Ever not quite!" — this seems to wring the very last panting word out of rationalistic

philosophy's mouth. It is fit to be pluralism's
heraldic device. There is no complete gener-
alization, no total point of view, no all-per-
vasive unity, but everywhere some residual
resistance to verbalization, formulation, and
discursification, some genius of reality that
escapes from the pressure of the logical finger,
that says "hands off," and claims its privacy,
and means to be left to its own life. In every
moment of immediate experience is somewhat absolutely original and novel. "We
are the first that ever burst into this silent
sea." Philosophy must pass from words, that
reproduce but ancient elements, to life itself, that gives the integrally new. The
"inexplicable," the "mystery," as what the
intellect, with its claim to reason out reality,
thinks that it is in duty bound to resolve,
and the resolution of which Blood's revelation would eliminate from the sphere of our
duties, remains; but it remains as something
to be met and dealt with by faculties more
akin to our activities and heroisms and will-
ingnesses, than to our logical powers. This

is the anæsthetic insight, according to our author. Let *my* last word, then, speaking in the name of intellectual philosophy, be *his* word: — "There is no conclusion. What has concluded, that we might conclude in regard to it? There are no fortunes to be told, and there is no advice to be given. — Farewell!"